Warrior • 108

Mau-Mau Warrior

Abiodun Alao • Illustrated by Christa Hook

First published in Great Britain in 2006 by Osprey Publishing, Midland House, West Way, Botley, Oxford OX2 0PH, UK

443 Park Avenue South, New York, NY 10016, USA

E-mail: info@ospreypublishing.com

A CIP catalogue record for this book is available from the British Library

ISBN 10: 1-84603-024-2
ISBN 13: 978-1-84603-024-6

Christa Hook has asserted her right under the Copyright, Designs and Patents Act, 1988, to be identified as the Illustrator of this work.

Page layout by Ken Vail Graphic Design, Cambridge, UK
Typeset in Helvetica Neue and ITC New Baskerville
Index by David Worthington
Originated by United Graphic, Singapore
Printed in China through World Print Ltd.

06 07 08 09 10   10 9 8 7 6 5 4 3 2 1

FOR A CATALOGUE OF ALL BOOKS PUBLISHED BY OSPREY MILITARY AND AVIATION PLEASE CONTACT:

NORTH AMERICA
Osprey Direct, c/o Random House Distribution Center, 400 Hahn Road, Westminster, MD 21157
E-mail: info@ospreydirect.com

ALL OTHER REGIONS
Osprey Direct UK, P.O. Box 140 Wellingborough, Northants, NN8 2FA, UK
E-mail: info@ospreydirect.co.uk

www.ospreypublishing.com

Artist's note

Readers may care to note that the original paintings from which the colour plates in this book were prepared are available for private sale. All reproduction copyright whatsoever is retained by the Publishers. All inquiries should be addressed to:

Scorpio Gallery,
PO Box 475,
Hailsham,
East Sussex
BN27 2SL
UK

The Publishers regret that they can enter into no correspondence upon this matter.

Author's acknowledgements

I should like to thank Funmi Olonisakin, Oyebisi Fawole and Ekaette Ikpe for their comments, and Martin Kimani and Zeedah Meierhofer-Mangeli for their assistance. It goes, of course, without saying that none of them is responsible for the contents of this book.

Dedication

This is to the memory of Benjamin Kyalo Mangeli, a Kenyan patriot and a specimen of a complete gentleman, who died just as the manuscript was being completed.

Editor's note

The Editor would like to express grateful thanks to Nicholas Wood and his father for their permission to reproduce their unique and previously unpublished photographs taken during the Mau-Mau uprising.

Cover image

Mau-Mau leaders in Kenya 1952–57. (Courtesy of topfoto.co.uk)

CONTENTS

MAU-MAU WARRIOR

HISTORICAL BACKGROUND

Although actual military activities lasted barely half a decade, the Mau-Mau revolt left enduring legacies on several fronts: on military history, where the oath of secrecy associated with the 'initiation' of combatants created a level of cohesion that proved crucial in military operations; on the politics of peasant revolt, where the sentimental attachment to land forced local peasants to take up arms against an imperial force that was militarily far superior; on the political economy of imperial rule, where the British colonial power brought an excessive firepower to bear on an unconventional force that threatened the grip of British imperialism in the heart of Africa; and on the sociology of intra-group relations, where undignified death sentences were inflicted on members of the local population who betrayed the common ethnic cause in the fight against what was seen as the feudal tyranny of imperial rule. Almost half a century after the end of the revolt, Mau-Mau continues to offer inspiration to a diverse range of people, from the Mugabe-endorsed 'war-veterans' fighting to regain land from minority whites in Zimbabwe, to others who saw sufficient fun in the rebellion to invent a game of cards named after the memories of this peculiar African revolt. There have also been novels and films on the revolt, with a former British Prime Minister, Winston Churchill, going so far as to narrate a prologue to one such film. But despite the wide use to which the rebellion has been put, what now seems certain is that the initial thinking, which portrayed the Mau-Mau revolt as a bunch of rag-tag forces that engaged in oath-taking, cannibalism and witchcraft, and dismissed the military activity of the force as being of mere entertainment value, is a gross misrepresentation. Indeed, it required the Lancashire Fusiliers undertaking the longest airlift in British military history, six battalions of King's African Rifles, naval forces, artillery, engineers, heavy RAF bombers and jet fighters to bring this somewhat irregular force into some form of submission, and even this took four years, at a cost of almost £60 million, a significant amount by 1950s standards.

But the Mau-Mau uprising has always been a peculiar revolt, with many of the issues surrounding it still shrouded in secrecy and confusion, even after

BELOW **A Mau-Mau suspect arrested for interrogation. Although arrested by black security agents, he will be taken to the white officers for interrogation. With the shortage of handcuffs, black security agents improvise with ropes to tie the suspect's hands. (Courtesy of topfoto.co.uk)**

50 years. For one, the origin of the word 'Mau-Mau' is not known. Some have associated the name with the numerous mountains bordering the Rift Valley, north-east of Lake Naivasha, from where the activists were believed to have sought and obtained inspiration and guidance in their revolt against imperial rule, while others have described it as a British coinage to ridicule the complex organizational structures of the indigenous military operation because of its somewhat unconventional nature. Still others argued that it was the acronym for *Mzungu Aende Ulaya – Mwafrica Apete Uhuru*, which translated from Swahili means 'Let the white man go back abroad so that Africa can get its independence.' Further still, some have traced the origin to a Kenyan clergyman who used the phrase on his pulpit to describe the African resistance to European control in the country. Whichever, it is noteworthy that those who formed the organization never referred to the group as the Mau-Mau. To them the organization was variously referred to as '*Muingi*' (The Movement) or '*Muigwithania*' (The Unifier) or '*Muma wa Uiguano*' (The Oath of Unity). There were also others who described the insurgence simply as the KCA, after the Kikuyu Central Association, the association that formed the impetus for the insurgency. Confusion over the meaning of the name apart, even the exact date of formation of the organization is still contested. While some put the date at around 1952, others have placed it around 1947, seeing it as the political heir of the associations that thrived in the 1920s when land problems were at their peak in the country.

But if the meaning and origin of the word Mau-Mau is uncertain, the aims and objectives of the movement were not. It was a revolt organized mainly by the Kikuyus, the dominant ethnic group in colonial Kenya, with some support from other smaller ethnic groups, particularly the Merus and the Embus, to challenge British colonial control. Land was at the centre of the Mau-Mau rebellion. Indeed, the movement was sometimes called the Land and Freedom Army. However, the true importance of this cannot be

appreciated unless the political, economic and spiritual significance of land among the sub-Saharan African population is taken into consideration. Land is, indeed, the most important natural resource in Africa, indicating not only a symbol of economic power, but also the spiritual link between the living and the dead. Consequently, the white settlers' massive acquisition of land that accompanied colonialism was seen by the African population as effecting a cut in the continuity between the living, the dead and the future generation, against which a war was legitimate. But as is often the case in wars against colonial rule, the target was not only the settlers but also the segments of the indigenous population who sympathized with them. This thus gave the Mau-Mau revolt the image of being not only a war against colonial domination, but also a civil war.

During the late 19th century, the European scramble for colonies in Africa had reached fever pitch, and the Berlin Conference had been convened to regulate colonization and trade in Africa. In July 1885, Britain declared a protectorate over Kenya. The formal opening of the East African Protectorate by the British in 1895 and the subsequent opening, in 1902, of the fertile highlands to white settlers, consolidated British imperial rule in the East African country.

While complaints against the land management policy of the British colonial government in Kenya were widespread, the Kikuyus were worst affected. Occupying the central highland part of Kenya, where the cool climate attracted considerable European settlement, the Kikuyus had had most of their lands taken over by white settlers, including the areas best suitable for agriculture. Indeed, by 1948, about $1\frac{1}{4}$ million Kikuyus were restricted to about 5,200 square kilometres, while 30,000 settlers occupied 31,000 square kilometres. The shortage of land forced many Kikuyus to become 'tenants' on European land, offering their labour in exchange for being allowed to occupy a patch of land. Over time, white settlers steadily demanded more days for the access they offered Kikuyu farmers, which the Kikuyus saw as a strategy for turning them into agricultural labourers. This deprivation was to be a crucial factor in the entire Mau-Mau revolt. Indeed, even before the Mau-Mau was formed, poor Kikuyu farmers who had moved to shanty towns around Nairobi after being dispossessed of their land by European farmers had begun harbouring anti-settler sentiments.

Land deprivation apart, a catalogue of other colonial policies also served to encourage the radicalization of African peasants during this period. These included the publication of the settlers' Kenya Plan in 1949, the crackdown on unions in 1950, the move to elevate Nairobi to city status also in 1950 and the official endorsement of the unpopular Beecher Report on African education in 1951. Also in 1951, when the British Colonial Secretary, James Griffith, visited Kenya, he was presented with a demand for the inclusion of 12 elected black members into the Legislative Council governing the colony's affairs. This request was rejected. Instead, Griffith proposed a council that ensured that the 30,000 white settlers had 14 representatives, the 100,000 Asians had six,

BELOW **White settlers in Kenya devised different methods of ensuring protection for their families from Mau-Mau insurgents. One such was the construction of bamboo sticks around residential buildings. (Courtesy of the Nicholas Wood Collection)**

the 24,000 Arabs had one, and the 5 million Africans had five, and these were to be nominated by the government. From the moment this proposal was made, the black population became convinced that a peaceful resolution of the socio-economic and political situation in Kenya was no longer possible, and extensive plans towards organized armed revolt against imperial rule were formulated.

Until recently, thanks to extensive research undertaken on the subject, most literature on the Mau-Mau has tended to trivialize the extensive and very complex military operation of the revolt. The activists have often been portrayed as a rabble of bloodthirsty cannibals, and the British military operation has been depicted as a triumphant expedition that intimidated the rebels into submission. Often ignored have been the political philosophy and the military machine that were deeply rooted in indigenous principles and tradition. This book addresses all the major aspects of the activities of the Mau-Mau warrior.

CHRONOLOGY

c.1947
It is believed that Mau-Mau was established and began holding meetings in the bush areas outside Nairobi.

1951
August: British intelligence report makes the first official confirmation of the existence of the Mau-Mau rebels operating in the country.

1952
8 April: Aguthi and Thenge locations of Nyeri districts punished with a fine of £2,500 for outbreak of arson.

26 July: First mass meeting of the Kenyan African Union (KAU) takes place in Nyeri.

24 August: Curfew imposed in districts in the outskirts of Nairobi where gangs believed to be Mau-Mau fighters have been setting fire to homes of Africans who refuse to cooperate with them.

7 October: A senior African chief who spoke against increasing Mau-Mau aggression is assassinated.

19 October: British government officially announces that it will be sending troops to Kenya to help put down the Mau-Mau revolt.

21 October: British colonial government declares a state of emergency. Jomo Kenyatta, the President of the KAU, is arrested for alleged Mau-Mau involvement.

30 October: Over 500 suspected Mau-Mau activists arrested.

14 November: 34 schools in the Kikuyu ethnic areas are closed down against the background of the Mau-Mau uprising.

18 November: Jomo Kenyatta charged with managing the Mau-Mau terrorist group and taken to the remote district of Kapenguria, where he is held incommunicado.

25 November: Mau-Mau declare open rebellion against British rule in Kenya; British government responds by arresting over 2,000 Kikuyu suspected members.

1953
1 January: Mau-Mau attack a remote farm in the Thompson area of Nairobi. Two settlers, Charles Hamilton and Richard Bingley, are killed.

2 January: Mau-Mau attack another farmhouse in the suburb of Nairobi. The occupants, Mrs Kitty Hesselberger and Mrs Raynes Simpson, are able to respond to the attack, killing the leader of the Mau-Mau group.

BELOW **The aftermath of a Mau-Mau destruction of an African labourer's farm quarters, with white police officers looking for evidence that could have been left behind by the insurgents. (Courtesy of the Nicholas Wood Collection)**

18 January: British Governor-General in Kenya, Sir Evelyn Baring, imposes death penalty on anyone who administers the Mau-Mau oath.

24 January: Mau-Mau capture headlines with the attack on the Rusk farm, killing Mr and Mrs Rusk and their six-year-old son.

26 January: Increased Mau-Mau activities and displeasure with government's response force European settlers to form their own commando unit. Government also announces that a new military offensive is to begin under Major-General William Hinde.

26 March: Major Mau-Mau offensives against the Naivasha Police Station and the Lari.

1 April: British troops kill 24 Mau-Mau suspects and capture an additional 36.

8 April: Jomo Kenyatta sentenced to seven years' hard labour in jail.

3 May: 19 Kikuyu members of the home guard murdered by the Mau-Mau.

8 June: British forces launch forest offensive against the Mau-Mau.

1954

15 January: General 'China', one of the key commanders of the Mau-Mau, is wounded and captured by British troops.

9 March: Two more Mau-Mau leaders, General 'Katanga' and General 'Tanganyika', surrender to the British authorities.

March: The British plan to end the Mau-Mau rebellion is presented to Parliament. General China, captured in January, is to write to other activists urging them to give up the rebellion.

11 April: British government admits that the General China strategy of the preceding month has failed.

24 April: Over 40,000 Kikuyu tribesmen arrested in coordinated dawn raids.

26 May: Treetops Hotel, where Princess Elizabeth and her husband were staying when they heard of King George VI's death and her succession to the throne of England, is burnt down by the Mau-Mau.

1955

18 January: The Governor-General offers amnesty to Mau-Mau activists. The offer is that they will not face the death penalty but will be jailed for their crimes. This is condemned by European settlers.

21 April: Two British schoolboys are murdered.

10 June: Britain withdraws the offer of amnesty.

1956

7 January: The official death toll for Mau-Mau activists killed in Kenya since 1952 is put at 10,173.

5 February: Nine Mau-Mau activists escape from Mageta Island prison camp in Lake Victoria.

21 October: Dedan Kimathi, the last of Mau-Mau field marshals, is captured.

1957

18 February: Dedan Kimathi hanged.

10 November: State of emergency is ended in Kenya.

1960

18 January: The Kenyan Constitutional Conference being held in London is boycotted by African Nationalist leaders.

1961

18 April: In return for the release of Jomo Kenyatta, the African leaders agree to take a role in the Kenyan government.

14 July: Jomo Kenyatta released.

1963

27 May: Jomo Kenyatta elected Prime Minister in Kenya's first multi-racial elections.

12 December: Kenya becomes independent.

16 December: General amnesty announced for Mau-Mau activists.

1964

12 December: Kenya becomes a republic, with Jomo Kenyatta as its first president.

POLITICAL PHILOSOPHY OF THE MAU-MAU WARRIOR

As in most wars against colonial rule, the Mau-Mau warriors had a political philosophy that guided their actions. It is, however, ironic that despite the extensive and sometimes complex nature of their struggle, the Mau-Mau warriors did not have this philosophy written down in any clearly defined document. There are a number of possible reasons for this. First, as stated earlier, the movement saw itself as the armed wing of a broader struggle that had a political agenda. Consequently, the task of propagating a political philosophy seems to have been left to the Kikuyu Central Association (KCA), with the Mau-Mau informing its members only that the movement and the KCA were the same, and that the guerrillas should consider the political philosophy of the KCA as corresponding to that of the Mau-Mau. Second, as in most struggles against colonial rule, caution may have been exercised in giving out too much information about the political agenda of the movement, such as could have been disclosed by the publication of a clearly stated manifesto. Although it was widely known that the movement was fighting for land and political freedom, other details that might need to be included in a clearly written political document may have been considered to place the movement's activities at risk, especially when considered in the light of the political atmosphere of the late 1940s and the early 1950s, when the propaganda effects of political manifestos of popular struggles were not fully appreciated. Despite all this, the movement did have a definite political philosophy that guided its activities and underlined its actions. It also had rules and regulations which often reflected these political principles.

What seemed to be at the centre of the Mau-Mau political philosophy was the conviction that land was worth blood and sacrifice. This conviction made two interwoven considerations central to the political doctrine of the struggle: the non-negotiable determination to regain their land from the white settlers; and the aspiration, through Kikuyu religion and society, of a level of discipline and cohesion among the Kikuyus in the pursuit of a common struggle. These two considerations were to underline all the activities of the group.

A number of key features come out as being prominent in Mau-Mau political philosophy. First, contrary to what is often assumed, the Mau-Mau warriors were not naïve enough to think that they could defeat the British imperial force. Indeed, a major political theme of the struggle was the need to let the British establish a dialogue to resolve the issues of land and of Kenya's political independence. For example, in August 1953, Dedan Kimathi, one of the leaders of the Mau-Mau, wrote a letter which was published in the *East African Standard*, in which he pointed out that only a political solution could solve the Kenyan problem. He specifically stressed that 'bombs and other weapons' would not work and that it was the 'responsibility of the

government to ... see the foundation of lawful ... peace and progress'. However, this aspect of Mau-Mau political philosophy has been subsumed under the general impression that the warriors were determined to attain their objectives only through the force of arms.

Second, the Mau-Mau wanted all the Kikuyu people to see the struggle as a collective effort at freedom. As will be shown later, several efforts were made to ensure cohesion among the Kikuyus, the most important being the swearing of oaths of allegiance to the Mau-Mau cause. While they accepted that not every Kikuyu could be a partisan oath-taking member of the Mau-Mau, they wanted to ensure that those who could not join the movement did not betray the common cause of the struggle. The organizers of the revolt realized early on in the struggle that there was no way the white settlers would have sufficient force, or the understanding of the local terrain, to meet the challenges of their rebellion unless they obtained support from the local population. It was this desire to ensure cohesion that explained the brutal killing of Kikuyus who were known to be sympathetic to the European cause and the whole idea of oath-taking, about which there has been much speculation and curiosity. There is, however, another dimension of the Mau-Mau political philosophy that may appear to be contradictory: although the Mau-Mau was against Africans who served as colonial supporters, the movement had the intention of forgiving these people after the struggle. Dedan Kimathi in a letter to one of the key leaders, Waruhiu Itote, better known as 'General China', noted that once freedom was achieved, all 'ahata, cia, buriri [loyalists, traitors and home guards]' would be forgiven. This is not as strange as it might appear on the surface, as it is based on the principle which seems prevalent across sub-Saharan Africa that once an 'outside' enemy had been defeated, 'members of the family' who had been led astray or intimidated to support the 'enemy' should be forgiven.

Third, the Mau-Mau espoused a political philosophy that indicated objection to anything that was representative of European colonialism and influence. Sometimes they extended this to somewhat ridiculous levels. For example, members were initially not allowed to drink European alcohol or smoke European cigars. This was designed to be an act of rebellion against foreign influences. The movement was, however, later forced to remove this code of conduct when it became a symbol through which the security agents identified members of the Mau-Mau. But, still in the pursuit of this anti-European sentiment, the group was determined to remove any structure that was thought to be important to the British establishment. This principle, for example, underlined the destruction of Treetops, the historic hotel where Princess Elizabeth and Prince Philip were staying when they learnt of the death of King George VI and Princess Elizabeth's accession to the British throne. With this destruction, the movement believed that they had destroyed something that was of considerable symbolic importance to British history. While they were not under the illusion that actions like this would send the settlers packing from Kenya, they wanted the white population in the country to realize that a new phase of demonstrative defiance had emerged in the protests against European control.

Fourth, the Mau-Mau rebels also placed an importance on Kikuyu civic virtues as a central issue in their 'manifesto'. From the very outset of the rebellion, there had been a vision of a struggle and a future Kenya that would be based on hard work and discipline. Consequently, there were efforts to separate those who did not share these passions from the hard core Mau-Mau fighters. These misfits were known by the Mau-Mau as *Komerara*. Indeed, Jomo Kenyatta, undoubtedly the best-known Kenyan nationalist of the period and the person most Mau-Mau combatants considered as their overall leader, had stated during the struggle that vagrancy and laziness do not produce benefit for a country. However, although in principle Mau-Mau had this position at the centre of its philosophy, seeing it through in practice was difficult, especially as many of those who joined the movement were politically ignorant refugees and press-ganged victims. Also underlining this civic virtue was the care-support the Mau-Mau provided for those who had fallen or had been in other ways affected in the course of the struggle. Money collected from members was also used to assist unemployed members and to pay legal fees for persons arrested on Mau-Mau charges. Later, after the emergency was declared, the wives and children of men who were arrested or killed were also given financial assistance.

Finally, the Mau-Mau warrior had it as a rule to try, as much as possible, to avoid killing women, regardless of the role they were playing in the struggle. There were two assumptions behind this principle. First, and more important, was that women, regardless of their ideological positions in the struggle, were considered as the 'mothers' who would produce future generations of Kikuyu youths. Consequently, deliberate actions should not be taken to deplete their number and thus deprive the ethnic group of chances of population increase. Second was the assumption that women were in passive agreement with the ideological positions of their spouses, and consequently the extent to which they could be held responsible for the view they took on the struggle could not be ascertained. It was thus considered unfair to punish them for what they did. While this was condescendingly patronizing, it saved quite a lot of Kikuyu women during the Mau-Mau struggle. This, however, should not be misunderstood as to mean that Mau-Mau soldiers did not kill women. Of course, as time went on, women became victims of Mau-Mau activities, but it is worth noting that there were philosophical principles that cautioned against the reckless killing of women, at least at the beginning of the struggle.

Essentially, in regard to the Mau-Mau political philosophy, three things need to be remembered. To begin with, the principles that guided the philosophy did change as events in the struggle dictated, and some of the issues identified here were those that were fairly consistent for most part of the revolt. Next, there were slight modifications in some of these policies from one sector of the rebel group to the other; and finally, the exigencies of war meant that many of these principles were ignored in the stark realities of battle. However, such principles were to have an effect and a role to play in recruitment.

BELOW **Jomo Kenyatta, regarded by many as the leader of the Mau-Mau. Indeed, many warriors looked up to him for leadership and direction. He became the first president of independent Kenya. (Courtesy of topfoto.co.uk)**

RECRUITMENT

In general, although the Mau-Mau relied largely on voluntary membership, which was not so difficult to obtain because of the extent of land deprivation prevailing among the Kikuyus during this period, there were also many people who were forced or tricked into joining the movement. The typical Mau-Mau warriors were young men, but there were also old men and women in the fold; certainly the majority of the forest fighters were illiterates or at most semi-educated, and usually they belonged to the poorer sections of the Kikuyu community, especially from the Nyeri District and Fort Hall.

The complex nature of the Mau-Mau revolt meant that there were many different layers in the movement, each one with a different recruiting procedure. Researchers into the activities of the movement have often divided membership into two: passive and active members. Passive members were often family members of the guerrillas who had left the towns for the forests to engage in the war. They were often young ladies and old women, and they were considered important because the latter could assist in transporting arms and food to the guerrillas without being detected, while the former could be used to entice members of the security establishment into providing crucial information about the movements and plans of the government security apparatus.

BELOW **A colonial officer and a member of the home guard watch as a Kikuyu woman is fingerprinted before she is issued with a pass-book that could enhance free movement. (Courtesy of the Nicholas Wood Collection)**

The 'active' members of the Mau-Mau were those who took part in the day-to-day activities of the movement, especially as active combatants. Those in this group are more difficult to categorize than the passive members. The decision to go into the forest to join the guerrillas is often interpreted as the commencement of formal association with the Mau-Mau. This is not necessarily the case. Membership of the Mau-Mau commenced the moment one took the oath of allegiance to the movement, which is not the same as simply joining the crop of fighters in the forest. Indeed, there were many different types of 'oathed' members of the Mau-Mau. First, there were those members who, after taking the oath to become members of the movement, were to remain in their employment, either because they were considered more relevant working 'under cover' at home, or because they had not been required to undertake operational assignments in the forest. This was one of the peculiarities of Mau-Mau membership, as members were told that they could contribute to the struggle from any sphere of life. Consequently, even after members had taken the oath of allegiance, they were not immediately (and sometimes never) forced to go into the forest to join the fighters. Thus, many middle-level workers in government establishments such as clerks, stenographers, typists and others were able to supply important

details about government plans to the Mau-Mau. Domestic servants of white settlers who had taken the Mau-Mau oath also contributed to the struggle by assisting guerrillas in gaining access to the private residences of the settlers when the activists came on raids. The recruitment of these 'warriors' was carried out by Mau-Mau groups in Nairobi. The activities of these people were to be very prominent in the Mau-Mau insurgence.

The second type of active members included those who were administered the oath of allegiance specifically with the intention of being immediately conscripted into the forest. This was often to meet specific manpower needs identified by different segments of the Mau-Mau forest armies. In this situation, the conscripts had no choice but to move directly to the forest and join the guerrillas. It was within this category that there was a high degree of conscription. The Mau-Mau fighters who were coerced were often captured at night and were initiated by the local underground Mau-Mau groups. As was to be expected, many of this group later fell to offers of surrender by the government, and became members of pseudo-gangs, seeking to overthrow the real Mau-Mau, as the revolt entered its most difficult phases after 1954. To prevent government agents slipping in, none of the recruits were told where they were heading and they were escorted under heavily armed guards all the way to the forest edge, thus guaranteeing that none of them turned back. At the entrance to the forest, all government documents, such as work cards and poll tax receipts possessed by the recruits were collected and burnt. New recruits were then taken to special locations where they were instructed for a day or two on how to use firearms. One such centre was Kassarani. After the training they would be escorted in small groups first to Thika, then to Fort Hall and finally to the Aberdare or Mount Kenya forests. The burning of their documents was to ensure that the new recruits would remain in the forest, for if they came out each knew he would soon be caught without documentation and immediately detained or shot by the government security agents.

The third type of active Mau-Mau members comprised urban repatriates who were driven to the

forest as much by hunger as by any other factors, and those who entered the forest out of fear of remaining in the Reserve, especially because of the collective punishment and general maltreatment imposed by the security forces. This proportion increased significantly after the declaration of the state of emergency, when the British colonial government embarked on massive repression of the Kikuyu populace. Often, these 'warriors' did not share the idealistic vision of the Mau-Mau, and unlike the ideologically focused fighters, they imagined that their stay in the bush would be temporary. When they realized that it could be a long haul, their interest began to wane, as they were not willing to exchange the hardship of the Reserve for another difficult life in the bush. The Mau-Mau groups in the forest in turn were cautious about the ideological credentials of these recruits, and many were subjected to rigorous interview when they arrived in the forest to ensure that they were not being sent to infiltrate the ranks of the guerrillas.

Next, there were members who had sworn the Mau-Mau oath but were not really intended to go into the forests, either because they were too old or because they had specific strategic roles that should keep them in Nairobi. These men played vital parts in many of the numerous committees formed to assist the activities of the guerrillas operating from the forest, acting also as suppliers of medicines and drugs. The importance and assistance offered by members in this category have often been underestimated, but it is clear that the guerillas in the forest could not have fought without the support of those operating at the background. This is, in fact, attested to by many of the Mau-Mau warriors who have written their memoirs since the end of the struggle. It is worth adding here that there were also individuals who were 'head-hunted' into membership of the Mau-Mau. These were people who occupied strategic positions within the government establishment and were considered to be of potential assistance to the Mau-Mau. They were won over through a number of ways, including bribery and entrapment by beautiful Kikuyu girls.

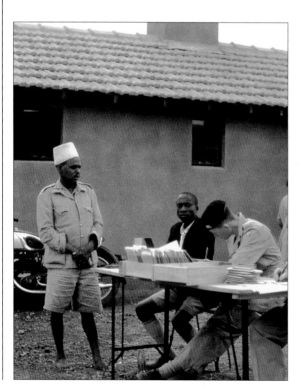

Finally, there were those who migrated to the forests at the beginning of the rebellion and who formed the *modus operandi* of the rebellion. The people in this category were few, and they were convinced of the justice of the struggle and the sacredness of their cause. They had, from the earliest part of the rebellion, been identified by the British colonial government, and some of them indeed had prices on their heads. Amongst these individuals were men like Dedan Kimathi, Stanley Mathenge and General China. They were later to welcome other members into the forest.

Right from the beginning of the rebellion, the Mau-Mau succeeded in obtaining the support of the oldest trade union in Kenya, the Transport and Allied Workers Union. The members of this union, especially the taxi drivers, played a very important role in the recruitment of Mau-Mau members. They used their cabs to transport oath administrators to the various districts outside Nairobi and return them to Nairobi before dawn. Even during the actual fighting, they continued to play a key role. For example, after a killing, they used their cabs to transport the fighters from the scene of attack to hiding places. The Mau-Mau also had an effective propaganda machinery for recruiting members, especially through local newspapers like *Inooro ria Gikuyu, Gikuyu na Mumbi, Wihuge, Wiyathi* and others.

As time went on and the membership of the Mau-Mau became popular, the movement introduced an ingenious device that brought in money for the cause. For example, latecomers into the movement, especially those who had previously demonstrated against the Mau-Mau, were made to pay a sum of money before they could become oathed members of the group. This income proved very helpful in the months preceding the declaration of the state of emergency.

STRUCTURE AND HIERARCHY

The structure of the Mau-Mau was constantly changing to meet military exigencies. This confused the colonial government into believing that the organization had no central administration. In fact, it took almost half a year after the declaration of the state of emergency before the government became convinced that a central structure controlling the affairs of the Mau-Mau actually existed. Another misconception that existed throughout most of the unrest was that the movement was controlled and commanded from the forest where the guerrillas operated. This was not correct. Indeed, the central control of the Mau-Mau for most of the war was held in Nairobi, where a civilian council controlled the activities of the group and passed instructions to the fighters in the forest through a complex network of structures that had been put in place by the Mau-Mau.

The first Mau-Mau Central Committee was formed at the beginning of 1953, adopting the name *Kiama kia Wiyathi* (the Council of Freedom). This council carried out its operation through three main groups: the first, a committee of six, was in charge of organizing the domestic, industrial and municipal workers; the second consisted of a number of African taxi drivers who were to ensure mobility; and the third was responsible for dealing with delegates from Mau-Mau district councils and committees. The Central Committee as described above was uncovered in April 1953, and 15 of its members were arrested. Another Central Committee was formed, which had in its membership one man from each of the main districts of the Kikuyu Reserves. Attached to this Central Committee was the War Office and Headquarters of the Army, whose chairman, known as the Commander-in-Chief, had the control, at least in theory, of all the Mau-Mau guerrillas. In practice, however, its task was more to collect recruits and dispatch supplies to the forests in Aberdare and Mount Kenya. There were also strings of committees. For example, under the Central Committee were other smaller committees representing every district in the Reserves; under this layer were committees representing every division in the district; and below these were committees representing locations in the division. In each case, the chairmen of the lower committees formed the next committee up. Meetings were held regularly, and each group had messengers whose job

ABOVE **Two Mau-Mau suspects arrested and being taken for questioning in the Aberdare forest, one of the main operating centres of the Mau-Mau insurgents. (Courtesy of topfoto.co.uk)**

it was to inform members of dates and venues of meetings. Predictably, most of these meetings took place at night. This structure, however, changed around September 1953, after several thousand guerrillas had entered the forest, when, with the constant pressure from the government in harassing members of the Nairobi-based committees, it was decided that the Central Committee should change its name and location. Consequently, the Central Committee became known as the Kenya Parliament, and more powers were given to the guerrillas then operating from the Aberdare and Mount Kenya forests.

The pattern of entry into the forest made it difficult for the Mau-Mau warriors operating from the forests to establish a clearly defined structure, at least at the beginning of the war. Fighters were recruited in two entry-phases. The initial entrants were those who were to form the core of the rebellion – people like Dedan Kimathi, Stanley Mathenge and General China and their followers, whose entry was relatively organized. The second phase, which was haphazard, saw the arrival of others, who came in as soon as they felt sufficiently bitter or concerned about their continued safety in the British clampdown. Most of these warriors entered the forest in an uncoordinated manner. People came in batches, and those who came together were often family members of people from the same locality; once they decided that they had had enough of living in the Reserve, they took a joint decision and migrated at the same time. In short, the activists were simply moving around in the forest without much knowledge of each other. One major consequence of the haphazard nature of such entry was that no one among the leaders could claim automatic pre-eminence over the others.

The first attempt to establish a formal structure was to form loose unions of groups who arrived in the bush about the same period. This was not particularly difficult, because of the close-knit nature of those entering the forest together. Leaders at this stage were selected on the basis of proven military and political capabilities, and the main duties of the appointed leaders were to provide food, protection and clothes and to ensure discipline. As would be expected in this context, the level of discipline and the structure of hierarchy varied from one place to the other.

In May 1953, the first district-wide military unit of the Mau-Mau was formed. This was the Nyeri District Council and Army, and it was at this meeting that Stanley Mathenge was appointed as Chairman and Head of the Army. In August 1953, through the initiative of Dedan Kimathi, the Mau-Mau forces in the Aberdares convened what was later known as the Mwethe meeting. This brought together military leaders who had led their independent units for about a year and were willing to surrender this independence. Not much success attended the effort to make these leaders surrender their claims. In the end the meeting formally recognized eight Land and Freedom armies, their commanders and their areas of operation. The meeting also created what was called the

Kenya Defence Council (KDC). Colonial literature painted Dedan Kimathi as the leader. This is misleading, as the struggle never had a supreme leader in the forest. Indeed, many actions taken by others were attributed to him, especially as he had become a mystical figure.

Immediately after the declaration of the state of emergency and the reinforcement of troops from England, the Mau-Mau did not know what their next line of action should be, and it took a month before they could figure this out. After the arrests that followed one of the government's military operations against the Mau-Mau (Operation *Jock Scott*) there was a period of confusion and the leadership of the Mau-Mau fell into the hands of those who lacked the political experience, education and knowledge of warfare necessary for the success of political revolution. In short, the Mau-Mau was on the defensive, reacting to the government's repressive measures.

For most of the time, the Mau-Mau operated a rank structure, with officers allocated ranks as in conventional military structure. The ranks were allocated by the military commanders appointed by the Mau-Mau war council. Most major commanders operated on the rank of general, with a very few, like Dedan Kimathi, having the rank of field marshal. The process of conferring ranks on other officers was often followed by a little ceremony, and the new officer might even receive an envelope containing a small amount of money or in some cases a promissory note of future payment, in the form of either cash or land to be taken from the white settlers. The promotion ceremony for more senior commanders was often more elaborate, involving calling on God to grant the newly promoted officer wisdom to carry out his tasks as a leader. Many believed such a ceremony was enacted when Dedan Kimathi left his rank as a field marshal to become the 'Prime Minister' and a replacement was made to fill the rank. Just as there were promotions, there could also be 'demotions' for guerrilla members who violated the rules. However, the extent to which these titles meant more than just symbols is uncertain, especially as guerrilla members were known to have been demoted rather drastically for misdemeanours that should have been effaced with mere warnings. For example, demoting a guerrilla from 'colonel' to 'captain' for being away from his command position, as was recorded in a memoir by veteran Mohamed Mathu, may suggest that these ranks did not mean too much in some cases. Mathu notes:

> One of our sentries was pushed into the room [where we were having an elders' meeting]. He had abandoned his post and gone to the nearby home of a woman-friend. The others tracked him down and now wanted to punish him. We calmed the man down and discussed the case at some length, finally deciding that since it was his first offence we would let him off lightly. He was demoted in rank from a colonel to a captain.

Self-styled titles were also common among the Mau-Mau leaders. As well as Kimathi, who used various titles including 'Field Marshal' and 'Prime Minister', other senior members had titles. For example, General Kahinga Wachanga, who at a later stage in the struggle led a section of the Mau-Mau in a negotiation with the government, gave himself the title, 'Colonial Secretary of States'. While all this can be dismissed by outsiders as ridiculous, it enhanced the whole concept of leadership and

ABOVE **Dedan Kimathi, undoubtedly the best-known of the Mau-Mau insurgents, after his arrest. He was later hanged for his role in the rebellion. Although he remained defiant till the end and maintained that he had no regrets for his role in the Mau-Mau, he died a staunch Catholic. (Courtesy of topfoto.co.uk)**

responsibility among the guerrillas. The fact too that the title-holder gained a sense of recognition and importance from such a title may have served as a source of encouragement at the battle-front. It is almost certain that many of these titles were taken to gain equivalency with colonial figures whose offices placed them at the forefront of discussions during the rebellion. It is also possible that people assumed them to give the impression that they were capable of holding such offices and discharging the required responsibilities in a free and democratic Kenya.

The nature of the Mau-Mau leadership is similarly intriguing. While most of the Mau-Mau members were uneducated and inexperienced, some of the leaders were battle-hardened, combat tested and fairly well educated. For example, some, like General China of the Mount Kenya forest, had fought with the British Army in Burma during World War II, while some had secondary education, which in colonial Kenya took them out of the category of illiterates. The leaders also commanded loyalty and respect from their troops and were known to have exhibited remarkable courage on the battlefield. Some of the leaders, including Dedan Kimathi, were charismatic figures and remarkable orators. While at the beginning they were frightened and avoided areas where they could be met with superior firepower, over time their confidence grew, and they confronted the security apparatus of the settlers with remarkable courage. There is also evidence that they could be very brutal in the ways in which they dealt with subordinates and with their victims. But what seems to be the most important characteristic of the leadership was their conviction in their struggle. Many of them remained resolute to the end, even when it was obvious that the outcome of their continued adherence to the Mau-Mau oath would be death by hanging. Dedan Kimathi, for example, maintained his loyalty to the Mau-Mau cause till the end, even though he converted to Roman Catholicism in his last moments.

OPERATIONAL RULES, PUNISHMENTS AND DAILY ROUTINE

Rules

All Mau-Mau members were to follow rules and regulations that were set by the command structure of the movement. By around 1953, the following were issued:

(1) No one was to be in possession of arms or ammunitions without the knowledge and approval of the Land and Freedom Army (LFA) Committee in Nairobi.

(2) No fighter was to carry his weapon unless on a specific mission; otherwise weapons were to be kept well hidden.

(3) If any fighter was arrested while he still had ammunition in his gun, he would not be given legal assistance by the Committee.

(4) No one was to take his weapons and join another fighting group without the knowledge and permission of the Committee.

(5) No fighter was ever to intimidate or threaten with arms any other member of the LFA.

(6) Any fighter injured in battle and unable to be moved to safety must be shot and not left alive for capture and interrogation by the government.

(7) No one was to drink European-manufactured beer unless obliged to while on official business, such as attempting to bribe an *askari*.

(8) No one was to smoke European-manufactured cigarettes, though the smoking of *karaiko* and *bhangi* was permitted.

(9) No one was to ride in European-owned buses.

(10) No one was to disclose any information concerning the LFA to any person not a member of the group, even if they were members of the Mau-Mau or fighters attached to different groups.

It can be added that, in case of Rule 6 above, before a wounded victim was shot, the maximum possible effort would be made to explain the rationale behind the decision to him and to obtain his consent about the decision to terminate his life. Memoirs of former Mau-Mau fighters have indicated that this was a very difficult moment, but that many wounded victims did endorse the decision by their compatriots to kill them instead of risking the lives of others in the attempt to get them to safety. Although there was no formal rule about this, most of the documents by former Mau-Mau fighters state that it was often someone from the victim's locality who would be made to carry out the unpleasant assignment of killing the victim. The exact reason for this is not known, but it probably demonstrated that the decision was unanimous, thereby preventing a possible break in rank of the guerrillas. Once again, the memoir of Mohamed Mathu records a vivid example of this:

[After the raid] I noticed that one of our men was missing. Glancing around I spotted Githongo lying on the ground a short distance away … I found he had been shot in the thigh. The bone was badly fractured. Kariuku was with me and we called over four men from the injured comrade's district. We quickly discussed the matter. We knew that within minutes the security forces would be swarming all over the place. Githongo couldn't move and we couldn't afford to carry him and thus endanger the whole group … The Fort Hall men [where Githongo came from] sadly decided that since Githongo could not be carried to safety or left to be captured and interrogated by Government, he would have to be shot. Githongo was then consulted and told about our decision. 'Do what you think best for the group,' he said, 'and leave quickly.' One of Githongo's Fort Hall comrades then put a revolver bullet into his friend's head killing him instantly.

Punishments

There were clearly cases of corporal punishments and brutality. There were no formal court systems, and committees of senior Mau-Mau members sat in judgement over cases of misdemeanours. For minor offenders, otherwise considered to be good members, punishments were usually fines or sometimes being beaten with the cane, but for more serious crimes, such as giving information to the government or regular violation of well-established rules, the punishment, of course, was death. The death sentence was also imposed on anyone who kept money sent to the forest for the upkeep of the troops. Trials were conducted by the officers; once consensus was reached about a man's guilt, he was accordingly sentenced, and this was carried out by a section that may be described as the Mau-Mau version of military police. However, the most serious offence in the Mau-Mau fold was betrayal, and any member caught divulging secrets to the government was killed, sometimes in the most brutal ways. Before this was carried out, however, evidence must have been established beyond any shadow of doubt and, in some cases, the accused would have confessed his guilt. Trial for this offence could take place anywhere, and there was one particular case where one of the Mau-Mau leaders, who had betrayed all his colleagues and informed the government of a major oath-swearing site, was arrested, tried inside a taxi-cab, and later strangled after 'conviction'.

Although there were attacks on homes of whites and black loyalists, raping of victims during such raids was strictly forbidden. Indeed, the raping of victims during a raid was an offence punishable by death, and the few Mau-Mau members who raped while undertaking military operations in the homes of black loyalists were instantly killed. This was as much a matter of moral principle as it was an effort to prevent the whole group involved in the operation from being 'polluted', and the entire military operation 'jinxed'. It is noteworthy that there was no reported case of rape of white females by the Mau-Mau warriors during the entire revolt.

Within the movement, there was no formal position on drugs, and many Mau-Mau warriors were known to be taking these. Many of the soldiers took marijuana, while there were also confirmed cases of soldiers chewing *miraa*, an amphetamine-like drug. While the white population claimed that these drugs encouraged the Mau-Mau soldiers to embark on reckless courage, one of the Mau-Mau leaders, General China, opined that the drugs were not used as stimulants for combat. Consequently, it was possible that the drugs calmed the men down before battle rather than aroused them to behave recklessly.

Routine

While in the forest, the Mau-Mau followed a strict routine. The wake-up time was 5:30am, after which the guerrillas were fed a maize-meal porridge (senior officers had the privilege of having meat

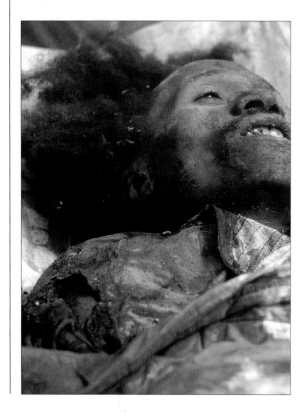

BELOW **A slain Mau-Mau leader. It was a common practice of the colonial government to display the photograph of any prominent Mau-Mau leader killed in the course of battle. (Courtesy of the Nicholas Wood Collection)**

and tea as well); after breakfast, whistles summoned the warriors for morning prayers followed by a parade call where men and women were assigned their duties for the day. Next, warriors performed calisthenics, marched, and were taught to lay ambushes, use cover, clean and fire their weapons and protect themselves during air raids. After the evening meal the warriors knelt facing Mount Kenya before being led in prayers that gave thanks for *Ngai*'s blessing and asked for victory over the enemy. Though there were small differences, the Mau-Mau warriors' prayer went along the following lines:

> Oh God of Mount Kenya, help us fight our enemies and don't let them take us by surprise. Help us win the struggle against the European by giving our fighters guns and ammunitions. Please, Oh God, protect Jomo Kenyatta and our other great leaders from the evils of the White man.

There were, of course, minor variations in some of the rules and regulations guiding the activities of the Mau-Mau, reflecting differences in leadership style and the vicissitudes of battle situations.

WOMEN IN THE MAU-MAU

One of the things that the British military mission sent to bring down the Mau-Mau rebellion found most surprising about the Mau-Mau was the use of women in active combat, perhaps particularly so as at this time the British Army did not use women in a combat role. However, women played many active roles in the Mau-Mau struggle, which though initially marginalized are now being widely recognized in academic writings on the struggle. Perhaps the most important role played by women who did not go into active combat was their support in terms of acting as go-betweens and carriers of food and firearms, as one of the strategies the colonial government adopted to weaken the morale of the rebels was to deny access to food to those in the forest. Indeed, stringent measures were taken to ensure that food rations to the Reserve areas were limited and well guarded. Kikuyu women were, however, able to circumvent these tight structures and to pass food to the guerrillas in the forest. Collecting food for the guerrillas was an important task that required centralized organization, and one particular woman, Wanjiru Nyamaturu, who played a most important role in ensuring a regular supply of food to the Mau-Mau guerrillas despite tight government regulations, was accorded the role of 'General in Charge of Food'. While delivering food supplies, the women also supplied key information about troop movements, official raids and possible informers.

Women also allowed their children, sometimes as young as eight years old, to be errand boys and

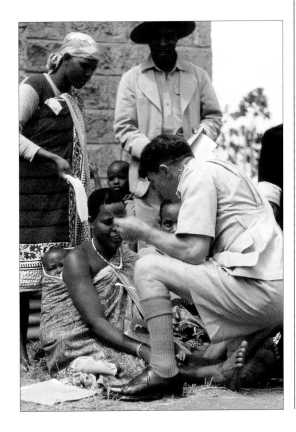

BELOW **Checking Kikuyu women for identification papers issued by the government to prevent the free movement of those suspected of being members of the Mau-Mau and their supporters. (Courtesy of the Nicholas Wood Collection)**

girls for the Mau-Mau cause. These children too were 'oathed', and they knew what to do and the language to employ in delivering the messages to the guerrillas. The advantage of this was that such small children were considered by the government security agents to be too young to be of any help to the Mau-Mau movement. Consequently, a young boy or girl seen on the road playing with his toy wheel might actually have been on an important intelligence assignment for the Mau-Mau cause. There were, of course, cases of children killed in the course of such assignments, and when this happened women also had to bear the painful mockery with which the loyalist soldiers would break the news to bereaved mothers. But despite all the hardship, women who did not join the active guerrilla force remained committed, and when they were caught by government security agents they withstood the tortures of their captors without revealing vital details about the Mau-Mau. Indeed, *The Times* of London noted the refusal of 60 women captured for carrying arms to reveal information about Mau-Mau activities.

As for women who took part in active combat, they constituted just about 5 per cent of the total guerrilla army. However, what they lacked in number, they made up for in commitment. Although initially women were made to play minimal roles as caterers for the camp, over time they obtained greater recognition and took part in active combat. In acknowledgement of their role, allowances were made to ensure that active women combatants were elevated to the rank of colonel. Women could also be elected to the Inner Secret Council, *Ndundu Ya Hitho*. However, before this could happen, they would have taken the oath of allegiance three times, as they reached increasingly senior levels, so by this point it was assumed that their loyalty and commitment to the Mau-Mau cause were unquestioned. Women also took other active roles. For example, there was a woman judge in the Mau-Mau court, whose duties could include passing death sentences on offenders, and it was reported that there were even women executioners. To some extent, though, promotion of women in the Mau-Mau struggle created a problem, as it was later alleged that those who were promoted, especially to the ultimate rank of colonel, performed other duties for the commanders beyond participation in active combat. For example, it was alleged that Dedan Kimathi promoted his sexual partner to this rank although she

RIGHT **Arrested Mau-Mau suspects awaiting questioning, with white officers deliberating. Some of these suspects are children. (Courtesy of**

topfoto.co.uk)

had not displayed sufficient military prowess. But this did not detract from the important role women played in the Mau-Mau struggle.

The involvement of women in the Mau-Mau cause is believed to have brought hidden tension to families where only one of the spouses was an oathed member of the Mau-Mau. Because of the nature of the oath, which made it mandatory for oathed members not to reveal their membership of the Mau-Mau to any uninitiated member, spouses were known to have carried out their obligations to the movement without informing their partners. While it was easier for men to do this, especially as not many men felt obliged to inform their wives about their activities, it was far more difficult for women to keep their activities secret from their husbands. Even where both husband and wife were members, tensions and difficulties did emerge in cases where the woman had risen to a position of authority in the movement and this was to affect her domestic duties as a wife and a mother, or when the woman decided to take the bolder step of going into the forest to join active combat. While an oathed man could not prevent his wife from joining the guerrilla force, the Mau-Mau made efforts to release some categories of women from military services. These included women with small children, and those who were pregnant or breastfeeding. The Mau-Mau also left a lasting effect on Kikuyu social structures. Many of the women who took part in the Mau-Mau movement no longer contemplated marriage after the end of the struggle, as they could not countenance the idea of playing a subordinate role to men as demanded by Kikuyu tradition.

MOTIVATION

Motivation for the Mau-Mau came from a variety of sources, perhaps the most important being their conviction of the justice of their cause. They believed that they were fighting on behalf of God, or *Ngai*, to remove the oppressors. They saw themselves as *itungati* (warriors). But they were also motivated by less ideological considerations. For example, there was the exuberance of young men thrilled by their new-found freedom in the bush, with all the attendant recognition they were getting from Kikuyu girls who often regarded with contempt those who had not taken the Mau-Mau oath.

Another major source of inspiration was the personality of Jomo Kenyatta, a British-trained Kikuyu leader who was seen as the hope of the nation. The position of Kenyatta vis-à-vis the Mau-Mau created confusion. He was the key leader in the Kenyan African Union (KAU), the association to which the Mau-Mau owed allegiance. Indeed, the general assumption was that the Mau-Mau was the armed wing of the KAU. To give the organization some image of respectability, it tried to publicly disassociate itself from the guerrillas, and on several occasions Kenyatta openly denounced Mau-Mau activities. The guerrilla fighters had no problem with Kenyatta's double image, and some were in fact thrilled by it, as they believed it served to further confuse the British as to the extent to which the KAU and the Mau-Mau were linked. Indeed, members of the organization considered Kenyatta's denunciations as being of mere entertainment value. However, ordinary members became confused when the tone of his pronouncements became stronger than they were used to. On one occasion, he described the Mau-Mau as having 'spoiled the country', proclaiming that it should 'perish forever'. What made this particular denunciation more disturbing to the Mau-Mau members was that it was in a public forum that he shared with the widely despised Chief Waruhiu. This was seen as having gone too far, and Kenyatta was called to order by the Mau-Mau central committees.

The Mau-Mau also had songs which motivated them in the course of the struggle. Many of these songs reflected their sufferings at the hands of the settlers, including their loss of dignity and the confiscation of their land. There were also songs that praised their past and present heroes, including Kenyatta and Koinange. These songs were believed to have strengthened them and inspired them to continue the struggle, despite the formidable odds against them. Some of the songs were evocative in both English and Kikuyu languages:

> Mother, whether you cry or not,
> I will only come back when our lands are returned;
> When I obtain our lands and African Freedom!

Other African groups engaged in wars of liberation were to follow this precedent of using songs as a source of motivation during their struggle. This was especially the case with *Chimurenga* songs during Zimbabwe's liberation wars.

Interestingly, the Bible was also a major source of encouragement for the Mau-Mau warriors. This initially appears a contradiction, especially when viewed against the people's deep-seated belief in traditional religion. There was, however, nothing contradictory in this in the eyes of the Mau-Mau warriors. Traditional religion and Christianity, especially the Old Testament section of it, were considered as being compatible, and Dedan Kimathi was known to keep a copy of the Holy Bible always with him. Indeed, while showing no remorse for his actions and defending the Mau-Mau cause fervently, he died a devout Catholic.

The troops were also spurred on by the presence of elderly men and women who came to the camps to give encouragement. During such visits, they advised the fighters of the justness of their cause and the inevitability of their victory. The guerrillas were also told of past battle victories of the Kikuyus, especially against the Masai and the Kambas, and were assured that the white settlers would soon be added to the Kikuyu list of victims. Subtle warnings also came with these words of encouragement, especially along the lines that the ancestors would be deeply upset if the youths did not fight to get back the lands that the white settlers had 'illegally' acquired.

MILITARY STRATEGY

As with most guerrilla forces, the Mau-Mau appreciated their superior understanding of the local terrain as their most important advantage over the colonial firepower, and selected their base accordingly. Militarily, the Mau-Mau operated mainly from two fronts: the Aberdare and Mount Kenya forests. This had strategic significance, as the two forests were, from the military point of view, some of the most difficult parts of the country to infiltrate and attack. The thick mountain forests with steep gorges and swiftly-running rivers provided perfect cover and almost impenetrable defences for the guerrillas. The fact that the areas were full of game animals also meant that the warriors were maintained with adequate food supplies when their supplies were cut off by government security forces. Indeed, the forests have been the traditional refuge of the Kikuyu in times of trouble. Even before the migration of the Mau-Mau, there were about 500 criminals on the run

LEFT **A Mau-Mau encampment destroyed by the police and** *askaris***. Because of their local knowledge, colonial police often worked together with** *askaris* **to locate and destroy Mau-Mau bases. (Courtesy of the Nicholas Wood Collection)**

living there. These were to swell the number of guerrillas who initially migrated to the forests. At the peak of the conflict, it was estimated that there could be between 15,000 and 20,000 Mau-Mau guerrillas operating from these two forests.

At the beginning of the struggle, it was estimated that the Mau-Mau had a little over 500 arms and about a quarter of a million rounds of ammunition. These were nothing compared with the enemy they faced. Indeed, all aspects of Mau-Mau strategy were predicated on their conviction that the enemy they faced was determined and powerful, and would employ all means to browbeat them into submission. Consequently, the details of Mau-Mau strategy involved ways of ensuring cohesion among their members and the intimidation and confusion of their opponents – the British colonial government and its African sympathizers.

There were eight key elements in Mau-Mau military strategy: the use, from a cultural point of view, of oath-taking; the place of magic in battle strategy; the intelligence network; the strategy of intimidation; the strategy to be adopted when arrested in the course of battle; the strategy of deception and taunting; the policy for dealing with traitors; and the place of sex in the pursuit of the struggle.

Oath-taking

Much has been written on Mau-Mau oath-taking, making this topic the most prominent aspect of the movement's activities. Oath-taking is in fact a relatively normal practice among Africans engaged in a common struggle, especially against a force believed to be strong enough to employ bribery and/or intimidation to break a group's resolve. It is a system traditionally employed to ensure cohesion and prevent treachery within the group. It was designed to make everyone to whom it was administered fear punishment by a supernatural power if he/she broke the oath. The roots go back deep into history, and examples have been recorded in several countries before and after the Mau-Mau revolt. Consequently, while the whole experience may be strange and uncommon in western societies, it is an altogether usual experience in sub-Saharan Africa. The primary motivation in Mau-Mau oath-taking was to ensure unity in the pursuit of a struggle identified as being common, and one they believed they were fighting not only for themselves but for future generations. The fighters believed that the colonial government would try to engage in divide-and-rule tactics, and therefore resolved to ensure unity through the employment of oaths deeply rooted in Kikuyu sociology, tradition and culture.

There were many oaths, each taken at different levels in the course of graduation in the hierarchy of the movement. Three of these were particularly important: the Batumi or first oath, taken at the first initiation into the fold; the second oath, taken after one had become considerably entrenched in the movement; and the leader's oath,

BELOW **A white officer inspects Mau-Mau initiation paraphernalia recovered after a raid on a Mau-Mau 'oathing' ceremony. (Courtesy of the Nicholas Wood Collection)**

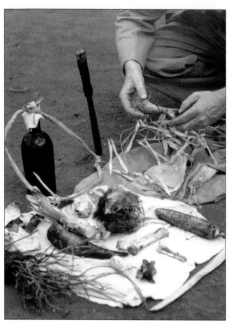

administered after a member had become a leader. The contents of the oath varied, but they were similar, as they called for serious retribution if the oath-taker failed to meet the required dictates. However, the entire process of oath-taking was inflated by the settlers and the Kikuyus from different motives. The settler community exaggerated it in order to convince the Colonial Office in London of the need to send troops to Kenya, while the Kikuyus further mystified the process to frighten the settlers and force them to flee. Some of the captured Mau-Mau guerrillas also concocted bizarre stories of what took place in the course of oath-taking in order to appease the government security agents. For example, statements claiming that the oath-taking involved pricking human eyes with a thorn, drinking menstrual blood, or eating the brain of a dead European were clearly exaggerations.

The process of initiation also varied, but in virtually all cases the process involved the killing of a goat, whose blood was then mixed with the blood of the people taking the oath. The blood was then spilt over banana leaves, from where it was tasted by the initiates. Presented below are the contents of the three oaths identified as being important in the Mau-Mau struggle.

For the Batumi, or first oath, there were six major steps arranged before the oath taker made the crucial pronouncements. First, the initiate would be required to remove his shoes and all the metal objects on his body, before being asked to pass seven times through an arch of sugar-cane stems and banana leaves. Second, a necklace made from special grass was put over his head. Third, he was given a piece of sacrificial meat and asked to eat it. This was done seven times, and between each mouthful the words of the oath were repeated. Fourth, blood was poured into the oath taker's lips. Fifth, a gourd with blood was passed seven times around his head, and, finally, the initiate was asked to pierce a sodom apple with seven thorns and insert a thorn seven times into the eyes of the sacrificial animal. The wording of the oath was as follows:

(1) I speak the truth and swear before *Ngai* and before everyone present here
And by this Batumi Oath of *Muingi*
That if I am called upon to fight for our land,
To shed my blood for it,
I shall obey and never surrender.
And if I fail to do so:

  May this oath kill me
  May this *thenge* kill me
  May this seven kill me
  May this meat kill me.

(2) I speak the truth and swear before *Ngai* and before everyone present here
And before the children of Kikuyu and Mumbi
That I shall never betray our country
That I shall never betray a member of *Muingi* to our enemies
Whether they be European, Asian or African.
And that if I do this:

May this oath kill me, etc.

(3) I speak the truth and swear before *Ngai* and before everyone
present here
That if I am called upon at night or during a storm
To destroy the house or store of a European or other enemy
I shall do so without fear and never surrender.
And if I fail to do this:

May this oath kill me, etc.

(4) I speak the truth and swear before *Ngai* and before everyone
present here
That if I am called upon to fight
Or to kill the enemy, I shall go
Even if the enemy be my father or mother, my brother or sister.
And if I refuse:

May this oath kill me, etc.

(5) I speak the truth and swear before *Ngai* and before everyone
present here
That if the people of *Muingi* come by day or night
And ask me to hide them
I shall do so and I shall help them.
And if I fail to do this:

May this oath kill me, etc.

(6) I speak the truth and swear before *Ngai* and before everyone
present here
That I shall never seduce the woman of another man
That I shall never take up with prostitutes
That I shall never steal anything belonging to a member of
the *Muingi*
Nor shall I ever hate or speak badly of another member.
And if I fail to do these things:

May this oath kill me, etc.

(7) I speak the truth and swear before *Ngai* and before everyone
present here
And by this Batumi Oath of *Muingi*
That I shall never sell my country for money or any other thing
That I shall abide until death by all the vows I have made
this day
That I shall never disclose our secrets to the enemy
Nor shall I disclose them to anyone not a member of the *Muingi*
And if I break any of the vows I have consciously made
I will agree to any punishment that this society decides to
give me.
And if I fail to do these things:

May this oath kill me
May this *thenge* kill me
May this seven kill me
May this meat kill me.

Many of the takers claimed that they experienced a miracle of conversion immediately after they had taken the oath. In the early stages oath-taking also served other social functions. It was a bond of camaraderie, with coded languages and signals. It was also a social symbol, as girls soon started discriminating against men who had not taken the oath. Over time, the contents of the oaths changed, reflecting the increasing level of militancy of the movement.

The process of the second oath was similar to the first. Herb leaves were dipped in a Kikuyu gourd containing a mixture of goat's blood, its abdominal dung and water, and this was sprayed on new initiates. The initiates then stood facing Mount Kenya to take the following oath:

(1) I swear before *Ngai* and before the people who are here that I have today become a soldier of Kikuyu and Mumbi and I will from now onwards fight the real fight for the land and freedom of our country till we get it or till my last drop of blood. Today, I have set my first step [stepping over a line of the goat's small intestine] as a warrior and I will never retreat. And if I ever retreat:

> May this soil and all its products be a curse upon me.

(2) If ever I am called to accompany a raid or bring in the head of an enemy, I shall obey and never give lame excuses. And if I ever refuse:

> May this soil and all its products be a curse upon me.

(3) I will never spy or inform on my people, and if I am ever sent to spy on our enemies I will always report the truth. And if I fail in this:

> May this soil and all its products be a curse upon me.

(4) I will never reveal a raid or crime committed to any person who has not taken the Ngero Oath [*Muma wa Ngero*, Oath of Violence] and will steal firearms wherever possible. And if I ever reveal our secret or fail to use or turn over to our warriors any firearms I acquire:

> May this soil and all its products be a curse upon me.

(5) I will never leave a member in difficulty without trying to help him. And if I ever abandon a member in trouble:

> May this soil and all its products be a curse on me.

(6) I will obey the orders of my leaders at all times without argument or complaints and will never fail to give them any money or goods taken in a raid and will never hide any pillages or take them for myself. And if I fail in these things:

May this soil and all its products be a curse on me.

(7) I will never sell land to any white man. And if I sell:

May this soil and all its products be a curse upon me.

As time went on, both the first and second oaths were administered at the same time.

The third oath was called the leader's oath, and, as its name suggests, it was given to those who were to become leaders in the movement. Standing in the middle of other members, the person taking the leader's oath faced the direction of Mount Kenya, raising his hands over his head with soil in his left hand and a piece of goat's meat in the right, and repeated the vow after the oath administrator:

I swear before *Ngai* and all the people here that:
(1) I will never reveal the leaders' secret to a warrior or any other person who is not a leader;
(2) I will never run away or surrender leaving my warriors behind;
(3) I will never abandon the leadership of my people but I will go wherever my people would send me and do whatever they ask me to do in my country's name;
(4) I will never degrade or criticize any leader in the presence of any warrior; and
(5) I will never by any means cause or plan the injury or death of another leader.

Each of these vows ended with the oath taker chewing some meat and a little soil and saying 'If I fail to do this may this oath kill me. If I lie may *Ngai* kill me.'

Other units of the Mau-Mau who were to perform other functions in the course of the war were required to undertake special oaths, reflecting the sensitivity of the assignment they were to perform. For example, those charged with relaying messages were known to swear a special type of oath committing them not to divulge any of the crucial information that was being entrusted to them. Again, it was possible to take a particular oath more than once, thereby reinforcing it.

Once the government recognized the importance of oath-taking and its binding effect, it initiated a process whereby those who had taken the oath would have the impression that they had been freed from the negative consequences of their earlier oath. The government then organized its own 'witch-doctors' to perform a 'cleansing' process that would 'de-oath' those who had taken the Mau-Mau oath. This process, known as the *gutahiko* ritual, was itself an oath-taking, in which the guilty party 'vomited' the Mau-Mau oath he had taken. Since the Mau-Mau oath was taken on the principle that the taker could not renounce membership, another ritual was designed to forestall the negative consequences that could follow renunciation. The government arranged for its own witch-doctors to perform this exercise. These witch-doctors were derisively referred to by the Mau-Mau as 'Her Majesty's Witch-doctors'. It is, however, important to point out that in the Kikuyu tradition there is no arrangement for 'de-oathing'. Once an oath has been taken, it becomes binding for life. Consequently, this arrangement made by the colonial government with the assistance of sympathetic black leaders to 'de-oath' those who had taken the Mau-Mau oath had no place in Kikuyu tradition and custom.

While the exact impact of oath-taking on military performance may never be known, what is beyond contention is that the oath created a level of bond and cohesion that was unprecedented in any struggle against European rule in Africa. Indeed, the colonial government appreciated the importance of oath-taking in the Mau-Mau struggle, and that was why tough sentences, including hanging, were prescribed against those administering the oaths.

Magic

Closely related to oath-taking was the place of magic in the Mau-Mau struggle. This, again, is a subject of intense curiosity to those who are not familiar with African culture. Even today, there are still many Africans, including those engaged in the armed forces of their respective countries, who believe that magical powers do play an important role on the battlefield. While it may have been overblown, it is indeed true that magic and witchcraft formed an integral part of the Mau-Mau battle strategy. In Kikuyu belief, God speaks through seers in dreams, and the seers, in turn, pass the messages to ordinary mortals. During the war, every Mau-Mau armed unit had magical powder and potions dispensed by *mundu muga wa ita* (the army medicine man), who also served as the chief military consultant. He gave consent before any attack was undertaken and also directed the route to take and the omen to avoid. The fighter relied on the predictions of the seers. Magical purification was also carried out at any time the leaders felt the need for it, especially when there were setbacks in military operations. Here the seer would bring together the members and perform a cleansing ceremony. The pattern of ceremony varied, but one method was for the seer to ask members to cover themselves with blankets, after which the seer (often a woman) would sprinkle contents from the stomach of a slaughtered goat on every man. Despite the extent of the Mau-Mau warriors' respect for prophets and seers, there were controls, and false seers risked painful death, just as genuine ones could be assured of enormous reverence. Of course, there were times where the seers got things completely wrong, but incredibly, there were cases when predictions were accurate. When things were wrongly predicted, seers were known to place the blame on the thickness of the forest which prevented the direct flow of instruction from God. It will, of course, remain a matter of opinion as to whether a successful prediction was the result of intelligent guesswork or actual celestial connection, or as to whether the seer had informants in government establishments who supplied background information that formed the basis of predictions.

But many Mau-Mau warriors combined the use of local seers with the employment of foreign charms. For example, Dedan Kimathi placed considerable faith in the *Napoleon's Book of Charms*, and allegedly spent a long time reading it and relying on it for guidance and direction. This may not be as contradictory as it might seem on the surface. Diversity in sources of spiritual support is not altogether uncommon in Africa, and tends to increase for those engaging in a struggle where loss of life is a distinct possibility.

Intelligence network

From the moment mass oath-taking began, the Mau-Mau employed an intensive intelligence network. The first element of this was the use of coded language to communicate amongst themselves, in order to avoid arousing suspicion and to ensure that messages were relayed without being understood by the uninitiated. For example, when an uninitiated member joined a gathering where discussions were taking place among oathed members of the Mau-Mau, a member would alert others by saying: 'Oh, there are fleas in this place.' This would alert other members to the infiltration, and discussions would change to another, safe topic. This practice continued, and was in fact perfected, after the guerrillas went into the forest. Coded languages were invented to describe government security agents. Some of these had their roots in the history and sociology of the Kikuyus or the antecedents of the various arms of the security establishment.

There were also signals through which Mau-Mau members communicated in the forest. Each Mau-Mau group had its own distinctive bird or animal call, and there were particular ways in which these calls were made. For example one of the groups used a signal imitating the *kanyuajui* bird. This would be made three times, after which there would be silence before it would be made again three times. There were also forest languages to ascertain credibility. At night, combatants identified themselves by the use of two names, *kalima*, the Kiswahili word for mountain, and *gitiku*, the Kikuyu for skin cap. Those who could not respond to one or another of these names were taken as enemies. Again, if a guerrilla returned to the forest at night, there was a coded language he would need to speak to validate his authenticity. Those arrested on suspicion of being infiltrators were also subjected to questioning by way of

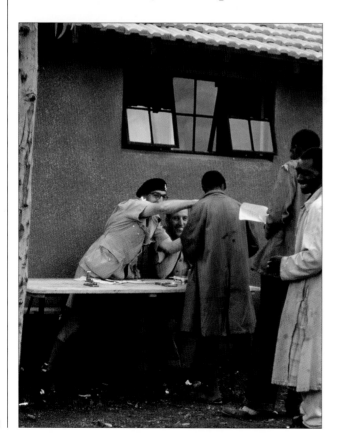

BELOW **Kikuyu men standing in a queue for identification passes. Before a person was issued with this card, the colonial officers had to be convinced that he or she had no affiliation with the Mau-Mau, but they frequently got this wrong. (Courtesy of the Nicholas Wood Collection)**

coded languages, and those who failed such tests were immediately identified as government agents.

There was a special body that was responsible for passing information among the numerous councils, committees and groups. Messages were often verbal or they were coded to be seemingly innocuous. The organization also penetrated virtually all segments of the colonial administration, with its agents having jobs in government offices, the home guard and European houses. There was also a section of its intelligence structure that specialized in forging documents for those who were to undertake specific tasks. In addition, there was a warning system: sentries were situated at regular points around the camp and they had a method of signalling the approach of the enemy by tapping trees.

Another integral part of the Mau-Mau intelligence network was the use of 'informers'. It was easier for the Mau-Mau to procure informers from within the government than the other way round, especially because of the poor wages paid by the British colonial government to African members of the security apparatus. Indeed, it was revealed years afterwards that many policemen, herdsmen and some prominent chiefs had taken the oath of unity to support the Mau-Mau cause. Furthermore, many administrative officers like clerks, telegraphists, typists and others were oathed members of the movement and they released the government's strategic plans, weapons and ammunition to the Mau-Mau. For example, it was afterwards discovered that a decorated veteran of the Burma campaign and a widely respected person in government circles, Paul Mahehu, was an oathed member of the Mau-Mau who acted as the liaison between the Mau-Mau and government employees. It was specifically noted that his exploits of infiltration and subversion boosted morale and significantly helped the Mau-Mau cause. Another remarkable Mau-Mau agent inside government circles was a man known as Njoroge the DO, who for a long time posed as a loyal district officer (DO) and gained the confidence of the government by repeatedly bringing poll-tax evaders and Mau-Mau suspects into police posts. It was unknown to the government that most of the people he brought in were loyalists, and that, in reality, he was escorting Mau-Mau guerrillas to the forest and delivering arms and ammunition to the insurgents.

Intimidating the settler population

Another strategy was aimed at instilling fear into the minds of the settlers with the hope of disrupting the way of life of Europeans in Kenya. By giving the impression that they could strike at any time and in any way, this strategy of fear achieved considerable success, at least initially. This early success was also due to the fact that the unorthodox nature of their philosophy and operation was such that the British intelligence took some time to understand the nature of the movement and the uprising. The threat was not only limited to Kenya. In a recently declassified document at the Public Record Office or, as it is now called, 'National Archives' at Kew Gardens, it was revealed that Mau-Mau fighters had threatened to take the war to Britain and to kill the wife of the British Prime Minister, Lady Clementine Churchill, as well as Lady Moira Lyttelton, the wife of the Secretary of State for Colonies, Oliver

Mau-Mau Warrior

Training Session

c

Prison Raid

D

E

Mau-Mau Trial

F

Lyttelton, if their demand for full independence was not granted. In this letter, written in 1954 and signed by a Mau-Mau activist who claimed to be based in London, the Mau-Mau wrote:

> Lady Churchill,
>
> This is a free warning to you. I as well as most of my ruthless gang will be out to shoot you dead any moment from now in Britain. End British atrocities … in Kenya now! Then live freely in Britain. I am demanding the withdrawal of all troops from Kenya within two month's time. … God truly knows that I have taken oath to fulfil this duty. It must be carried out. We are also sure that Mrs Lyttelton's life is at present not safe too.
>
> Yours most wickedly,
> General Stalin

While there was never any reason to believe that Lady Clementine's life was ever in any serious danger, letters like the above indicate the extent to which the Mau-Mau believed in the justice of their cause to free the country of British rule and their right to extend their war to the personal lives of those they considered to be at the helm of British colonial control.

For the settlers living in Kenya, however, the threats of the Mau-Mau were very real. Every white settler in Kenya had at least one Kikuyu servant, cook, garden boy or chauffer, and they were in positions where they could kill their white master, either through poison or in a direct physical attack, if they were so instructed by the Mau-Mau. There was, indeed, a time when the possibility of mass-poisoning was rumoured among the white community in Kenya.

Strategy when arrested

To guard against an arrested Mau-Mau implicating and endangering the lives of others, the organization decided on a procedure to be followed if a member was captured and interrogated by the police. As guerrilla members who had not confessed after being arrested were known to have been killed, it was agreed that members should prepare themselves for a simple, harmless and misleading confession in the event of an arrest. The arrested guerrilla was to say: (a) he was forcibly administered the Mau-Mau oath; (b) the area of administration was unknown to him, as he was taken there at night blindfolded; and (c) the oath administrator and others present at the oath were total strangers to him. Over time, some Mau-Mau members added their own ingenuity to this line of action by citing the names of those who had already been killed as their oath administrators.

Mau-Mau warriors also perfected a strategy of bribing some white troops with money to secure freedom for captured friends. This is an aspect of the conflict that is not widely known but memoirs written by former Mau-Mau fighters have shown that at a later stage of the war there were clear understandings between some white officers and the Mau-Mau. The officers implicated in this bribery allegation were not part of those who came into the country specifically to address the insurgency, but white officers who were born and had lived in Kenya before the revolt. Another veteran, Karigo Muchai, notes in his memoir:

> Many Europeans took advantage of situations created by Mau-Mau and became rich men. Some through bribes and theft, others through the sale of firearms and ammunitions to our agents. This corruption is not widely known and is never talked about in European or Government circles.

There was also a strategy to be adopted when a captured comrade was released or escaped captivity. It was felt that the loyalty of such people should be reconfirmed, as it was possible that they had traded their safety for becoming informants of the government. Consequently, such a person was put under close observation for some time before being allowed to take up his former position within the organization.

Deception and taunting
There were also attempts to confuse the government into believing that the Mau-Mau had spread to other Kenyan ethnic groups. For example, in October 1953, a letter was written to the *East African Standard* appointing one General Ogutu, of the Luo ethnic group, as the coordinator of non-Kikuyu members, and instructing that all non-Kikuyu members must work closely with him. There was, of course, no General Ogutu, and the Mau-Mau had not extended beyond their traditional Kikuyu enclave.

ABOVE **A black Kenyan having his photograph taken after procuring an appointment with the colonial government. While there were genuine employees, many of those who took up government employment had taken the Mau-Mau oath, and were releasing information about the government's plans to the rebels. (Courtesy of the Nicholas Wood Collection)**

Another related strategy was that of taunting. For instance, during the early days of the rebellion, it was not uncommon for Mau-Mau soldiers to send letters taunting the British colonial government. One such letter was sent in July 1953, by Henry Kahinga Wachanga to Governor-General Baring and General Erskine, with the news that the Mau-Mau were building a can factory to be used for canning the flesh of the defeated British. Another letter was sent by General Kago, a Mau-Mau general, to the British military commander promising him that Mau-Mau troops would spend the night within 200 yards of a British military camp, and the following morning Kago wrote to the British commanding officer thanking him for his 'hospitality'. It is very unlikely that the British authorities took these seriously; possibly the Mau-Mau guerrillas realized this, but nevertheless sent their messages to lighten the boredom of having to live in the forest.

Dealing with traitors
The Mau-Mau identified African support as being crucial to European success. Their strategy was thus to break the backbone of local support for

ABOVE **Checking farm labourers for possible Mau-Mau associations. These interrogations were often carried out by white officers who were proficient in the Swahili and Kikuyu languages. (Courtesy of the Nicholas Wood Collection)**

the white settlers. To do this, Africans who supported white settlers were killed in manners that were thought to serve as deterrents to any who might contemplate betraying the Kikuyu cause. The killing of these people was also meant to send signals to the colonial masters that the Mau-Mau activists were willing to embark on violence against civil authority. Indeed, a number of prominent Kikuyu chiefs sympathetic to the white cause were killed. Perhaps the most prominent of these was Senior Chief Waruhiu, who was not only a known supporter, but was also one of the organizers of the purification ceremonies meant to psychologically free those who felt they had been forced into oath-taking from supernatural retributions. On his way home from a meeting on 7 October 1952, he was shot four times at close range. It was the killing of Chief Waruhiu that speeded Governor-General Baring into imposing the state of emergency.

The place of sex in the struggle

Sex became a contentious issue for Mau-Mau guerrillas, especially as most of the fighters were young and unmarried and were at the age when sex was an important issue. At the beginning of the revolt, what seemed to be the dominant view was that marital relations were incompatible with life in the forest. Indeed, the opinion of some of the key leaders was that such a relationship was meant for the 'normal world'. This apart, a number of other considerations made sex a contentious issue. First, it was thought that the enemy could penetrate the camp and seduce the leaders through tempting sexual advances by women. This was not an experience limited to Kenya. Even in post-independence popular struggles, the possibility of sex being used to gather information to be used by opponents against leaders was a key factor. The Mau-Mau knew this quite well as it was a strategy the movement had itself used to elicit information from the home guards and other security agents. Second, it was believed that many of the local charms being used by the guerrillas would lose their efficacy if the partaker engaged in sexual acts. Indeed, Mau-Mau fighters who visited their wives in the Reserves were made to undergo cleansing on their return to the forest. Third, there was the assumption that sexual intercourse – especially when had regularly – physically exhausts men. It was also believed that it diverted the minds of the guerrillas from the more serious business at hand. Sex was therefore seen as being somewhat incompatible with active military service. Finally, the guerrilla force had to contend with the issue of ratio, as there were very few women to the numerous men in the forests.

There was no uniform policy on the attitude to sex in the forest as there were, indeed, divisions among senior members on this topic. While there was no question of enduring relationships in the forest, some senior members, including Dedan Kimathi, did not subscribe to total abstinence.

In January 1953, at a meeting of some area commanders, it was decided that unenforceable celibacy should be replaced with regulated cohabitation. Indeed, it was believed that Kimathi abused his own rules by allegedly abducting women food suppliers. This was to affect camaraderie among the fighters, as many of his able commanders, including Colonel Wamugunda and General 'Knife-in-the-buttocks' Kahiu-Itina, accused Kimathi of sexual wrongdoings. Kimathi's private failing along sexual lines was to have fatal consequences. First, there were allegations that he refused to punish his brother, Wambararia, for supposedly trying to murder his sexual rivals. But, just as this was convincing people of his partiality, he ordered the public flogging of a fighter of lower rank ostensibly for sleeping with a woman. It was this fighter, feeling publicly humiliated, who allegedly betrayed him to the Kenyan Police.

The Mau-Mau, though, did use sexual allure to their advantage as attractive girls sometimes used their beauty to lure African traitors, soldiers or policemen into traps, and the Kikuyu Commercial Sex Workers (prostitutes) sometimes demanded rounds of ammunition for payment when offering their services to members of the security establishment.

MAU-MAU WEAPONS

Like many aspects of the Mau-Mau revolt, the nature and sources of the organization's weapons were subjects of considerable speculation and interest. Whatever the speculations, it is now established that, contrary to the assumption at the time, there were no weapon supplies from the Communist world. It is likely that the theory of a Communist connection arose largely because the sources of weapons for the organization were unknown. Indeed, virtually all the weapons used by the activists were homemade, and the impression of external supplies of arms was rooted in the determination exhibited by the activists.

Guns were the most important weapons available to the Mau-Mau warriors, although they possessed few of them. It is now believed that efforts to secure guns had begun as early as 1949, and even by then Kikuyus had begun training young recruits on how to use the weapons. Word had, indeed, gone round as early as this time that all Mau-Mau members should try to secure guns using all means possible. There were three main ways in which Mau-Mau fighters obtained their guns: stealing, buying and voluntary giving from the government's security agents. Stealing was achieved by apprehending government security agents, who were often attacked when found in isolated places. It was, indeed, a common practice to spy on lonely policemen

BELOW **Mau-Mau suspects waiting to be questioned for alleged involvement in the insurgence under the watchful eyes of an armed member of the home guard. (Courtesy of the Nicholas Wood Collection)**

ABOVE **During the war, Mau-Mau insurgents sometimes displayed notices to warn their fellow Kikuyus of the consequences of betraying the Kikuyu cause and supporting the colonial government. (Courtesy of topfoto.co.uk)**

with guns; depending on their mood and the level of resistance from the victims, the activists might kill the policemen. This forced the government to strengthen police patrol teams. There were also cases when prostitutes were used to tempt home guards to secluded areas, where they could be attacked and their weapons seized. In addition, raids were conducted on prisons and security posts from where guns and ammunition were stolen. For example, during the raid on the Naivasha Police Station in March 1953, the Mau-Mau arsenal benefited from 29 rifles, 18 automatic weapons and an undetermined amount of ammunition, which constituted a major acquisition for the Mau-Mau.

Guns were bought from two sources: government security agents and Asian businessmen. The Mau-Mau were able to acquire money to purchase weapons by gathering the money collected from oathing fees, from fines assessed on late-coming initiates and from collections from local members. Because of the low salaries paid to security agents, it was quite common for home guards to sell their weapons for supplementary income and to go back and complain to the government that their weapons were taken from them during a Mau-Mau attack. Memoirs written by Mau-Mau veterans have shown that Asian businessmen and their European partners also sold arms to Mau-Mau. One of the veterans, Ngugi Kabiro, notes:

> When I left Kinyua, I went immediately to see my Asian friend. Telling him what I needed, we arranged to meet a few days later on Latema Road in front of the Green Hotel. He was to bring me six pistols and some ammunition for an agreed price of 800 shillings ... On the appointed day I was waiting in front of the Green Hotel when the Asian drove up in his car. With him was a European whom I'd seen earlier in the shop. They were obviously partners and, though a little concerned at seeing a white face, I wasn't really worried ... I approached the Asian, [checked] the contents of a sack in the trunk of his car while his partner sat poised behind the wheel. Seeing that the six pistols and ammunition were there ... I gave the money to the Asian.

This desperate desire to acquire guns also offered opportunities for Mau-Mau guerrillas to make a little money for themselves by inflating the amount of money they had spent in procuring guns from government security agents or the Asians. This strain of narrow interest did not, however, infect everyone.

The third source was the voluntary loaning of guns by home guards who had become oathed members of the Mau-Mau. Nairobi was a main source of weapons for the insurgents. From here, arms were transported through Kaimbu District, where local committees of the movement played a critical role in ensuring that the weapons got to the guerrillas in the forest. The Mau-Mau also had a factory where men produced guns that were used in battle.

The insurgents also used spears. These were the first weapons used by the movement, and they were manufactured largely by local blacksmiths. Other local weapons included *simis*, which are long-swords, *kibokos*, which are rhino-hide whips, and *pangas*, a type of machete made of soft irons.

In most cases, Mau-Mau warriors reacted well to the weapons they were using and they felt comfortable using them. They were sometimes disappointed, though, that some of the locally made guns often failed to work at crucial times.

MILITARY OPERATIONS

In their actual military operation, the Mau-Mau guerrillas were arranged in three main sections: the Aberdares forest section, the Mount Kenya forest section and the Nairobi section. The operational areas of the first two were the three districts of the Kikuyu land unit, namely Kisumbu, Fort Hall and Nyeri, as well as the territories around Nakuru, Nanyuki and Thika. The Nairobi section operated around Nairobi, especially around the city and Kaimbu. The troops in the Aberdares and Mount Kenya forests were divided into 'battalion' types, comprising between 300 and 500 men; smaller fighting units called 'companies' had around 100–250 men, and platoons had 50–100, while sections had between 10 and 50.

At the beginning of the Mau-Mau activities, efforts were made to avoid direct confrontation with either the British imperial force or the home guard. This strategy was predictable against the background of the enormous firepower at the disposal of the colonial force. The typical Mau-Mau military operation initially was to attack white farms, especially those in secluded areas. Many of the farm-owners did not realize that several of their domestic staff had become passive members of the Mau-Mau. This was not particularly surprising, as, while many of the whites were kind and considerate to their black staff, there were those who grossly maltreated them, treating their employees as no better than hired chattels. During the revolt, the task of these domestic staff was to supply key

BELOW **A young *askari* guard with his bow and arrow, again attesting to the importance of this category of weapon during the Mau-Mau uprising. Since there was a shortage of guns, *askaris* preferred to use weapons with which they were quite familiar. (Courtesy of the Nicholas Wood Collection)**

information about the movements of their masters and then grant access to the Mau-Mau activists when they chose to attack.

The year 1953 marked the beginning of real Mau-Mau activities. Right from New Year's Day, a pattern of attacks on whites began. On the first day, the domestic servant of a white settler, Charles Hamilton Ferguson, admitted a gang of Mau-Mau into his residence just as he and another white settler, Richard Bingley, were about to have a late evening dinner. Both men were killed. The following day, there was an attack on another farmhouse, belonging to Mrs Kitty Hesselberger and Mrs Raynes Simpson. The pattern of attack was similar, with the house-help allowing a Mau-Mau gang to gain access to the property during the evening. After the previous day's incident, white settlers were armed and prepared for possible attacks. When the houseboy entered the house in a suspicious manner, Mrs Simpson intuitively picked up her gun before

An *askari* employed as a private security guard by a white farmer practising with bow and arrow. Although crude in appearance, the bow and arrow was an extremely effective weapon used during the Mau-Mau rebellion. (Courtesy of the Nicholas Wood Collection)

the Mau-Mau gang came in. She was thus able to kill the leader of the group with her first shot. Mrs Hesselberger also managed to pick up her gun and shot and wounded some other Mau-Mau members, who all came in armed with *pangas* and machetes. There were very few guns at this time, and Mau-Mau guerrillas often ran away the moment they realized that their victims were armed with guns.

The Mau-Mau atrocity that brought the reality of the new insurgence home to white settlers took place on 24 January 1953, when Mau-Mau activists attacked the home of a white settler, Mr Rusk. Here, again, it was the same pattern: his house-help had connived with Mau-Mau activists who came into the Rusk farm at about 9pm. Both Mr and Mrs Rusk were killed and their bodies mutilated. What, however, brought the incident to the fore of global attention was that this Mau-Mau group also killed the couple's six-year-old son, Michael, who was then in bed.

In the light of the relative success that attended their policy of intimidation, the Mau-Mau modified their activities towards the end of March 1953, when the movement launched its first major offensive against colonial rule in Kenya. This was the raid on Naivasha Police Station. Viewed against the initial policy of attacking sites with minimal risks, the attack on the police station went against the Mau-Mau tactical pattern. The police station had everything that should caution against any attack on it by the Mau-Mau. For example, the place was of significant communications importance, where a major road junction and the railway came together. Moreover, the fence surrounding the station had been further reinforced with barbed wire. At about 9pm,

BELOW *Askari* guards employed by a local white farmer. With increasing Mau-Mau activities, especially on isolated settlements, white farmers employed local people as security guards. Over time, however, some of these guards became 'oathed' members of the Mau-Mau and ended up betraying their employers. (Courtesy of the Nicholas Wood Collection)

nearly 90 Mau-Mau rebels invaded the police station, attacking the police officers on duty. The officers could not offer any meaningful resistance and fled to safety. At the end of the operation, the Mau-Mau activists killed two policemen and freed about 180 prisoners, as well as escaping with some weapons. The operation was completed within 20 minutes without any Mau-Mau casualties. Just as this was going on, another Mau-Mau operation was being conducted in another location about 25 miles north-east of Nairobi in an administrative area called Lari. The people living in the area were known to be predominantly anti Mau-Mau, and many of the men belonged to the Kikuyu Home Guard. The attack on Lari was predicted by the colonial intelligence as early as 18 March, and a detailed defence plan was put in place to meet the envisaged attack. This included a company of King's African Rifles (KAR) assigned to major defensive positions. However, the company received orders from Nairobi to redeploy on 26 March, in order to avert anticipated trouble at the Athi River prison, approximately 40 miles to the south. The local home guard detachment of 150 men was out on patrol in the forest, rather than guarding the perimeter, when the Mau-Mau force estimated at 1,000 men moved into attack positions. The positions had been spaced along the entire 11-mile stretch, enabling all homesteads to be attacked simultaneously. The force was subdivided into attack units, each of which was assigned a specific homestead. Each attack unit was composed of three sub-units with specific tasks: one sub-unit bound the huts with cable to prevent the doors from opening, another soaked the huts with fuel and ignited them, and the third attacked fleeing victims who managed to escape the flames. The official count of Kikuyu dead was 84, but many corpses were so completely hacked apart and scattered around that the count was questionable. There were only 31 survivors, all of whom were badly wounded. Because many of the male inhabitants were out on patrol with the home guard, two-thirds of the victims were women and children. Over 200 huts were burnt and approximately 1,000 cattle were maimed in the attack. The operation was believed to have been led by Dedan Kimathi.

The Lari incident was one of the most controversial raids during the entire Mau-Mau struggle. The guerrillas claimed that most of the atrocities were carried out by government security agents impersonating Mau-Mau, while the government decried it as one of the inhuman activities of the Mau-Mau against their own Kikuyu people. On the whole, attacking Lari did more damage than anything else for the Mau-Mau, as it turned the population against the movement. Mau-Mau activities continued afterwards, however, operating hit-and-run attacks against white settlers.

As the war went on, criminal elements inevitably crept in. These elements, known as *Komerara*, operated in small gangs on the edges of the forest, robbing local inhabitants and masquerading as Mau-Mau. There was speculation that some of them were in the pay of the government, but many of them were independent entrepreneurs who saw an opportunity and went for it. However, by 1955 genuine Mau-Maus were raiding the Reserves for food. This annoyed the passive wing of the movement, and cracks began to emerge in the arrangement.

Whenever any member of the security forces, especially the home guard, was killed, his arms and clothing were taken by Mau-Mau fighters. This, according to Mau-Mau veterans, was done because the arms and uniform were badly needed, and they proved very useful in the Mau-Mau deception of the security forces. One of the Mau-Mau veterans explained how crucial these items could be:

In December 1953 some of our men were arrested and taken to the police post. Putting on a metal home-guard armband I had

BELOW **Members of the home guard receiving instruction from an officer of the colonial government. These home guards played a very important role in the war against the Mau-Mau, and they were most hated by the local population. (Courtesy of the Nicholas Wood Collection)**

acquired, I walked right into the post where the men were being detained. There I found a European officer whom we called '*Muru wa Waitana*' or 'Son of the Fat-man', a nickname he achieved because of the size and shape of his father. He spoke Kikuyu very well, and I told him I was a home guard from a nearby post and that I'd heard that six of my relatives had been arrested. I said that the men were all decent people and had nothing to do with Mau-Mau. Muru wa Waitima replied that the men stood a good chance of being detained or even killed and that it would cost me a thousand shillings to gain their release. Knowing this might happen I had brought with me a large sum of money. I paid the European the bribe he demanded and walked out freely with my six comrades. Soon we parted ways, the six men returned to their work in the forest as I made my way back to report the incident to the committee.

As would be expected in a war of this nature, there were cases of savage and sadistic killings by the Mau-Mau warriors. But these were not as profound as they were often made out to be. From the official records of Mau-Mau victims taken to the hospital for post-mortems before June 1954, just between 2 and 3 per cent were killed by burning, while about 5 per cent were strangled. Over 90 per cent were said to be killed by gunshots or *panga* wounds. A common method of Mau-Mau killing was a blow to the head. Indeed, so common was this means that a British pathologist who examined the bodies of alleged Mau-Mau victims came to the conclusion that the Mau-Mau had been specifically trained to kill their victims by this method. But there were also remarkable acts of kindness sometimes demonstrated by the Mau-Mau towards their victims, especially whites. For example, in December 1954, a British woman, Mrs Carnelley, and her two sons were spared after Mau-Mau guerrillas attacked her house. Although Mrs Carnelley fought back and indeed fired one shot before her rifle jammed, an action which could

RIGHT **The aftermath of a Mau-Mau attack. Attacks such as this often happened in the night, and they were frequently carried out against black members of the security forces. (Courtesy of the Nicholas Wood Collection)**

have qualified her for instant death, she and her sons were allowed to live, though on the condition that she left Kenya for Britain by the first available plane.

The Mau-Mau's selection of their military targets was sometimes devoid of strategic and political logic. This was particularly the case with their attacks on mosques. While there was nothing in their political philosophy that was inherently anti-Islamic, some members believed that Nairobi Muslims were using their magical powers to assist the government against the Mau-Mau. It was thus decided that attacks should be made on mosques. Armed with guns, five rifles and a pistol, an attack was launched on Eastleigh Mosque at night, with eight people killed. Another attack on Pumwali African Mosque a week later gave the impression that the first incident was not a mistake, and that the Mau-Mau intended to target Muslims. This was to remain one of the most curious aspects of the Mau-Mau revolt.

BRITISH RESPONSE TO THE MAU-MAU INSURGENCY

It took colonial intelligence quite some time before they knew about the Mau-Mau, and, even after they became aware of the movement, considerable time elapsed before the full security implications were appreciated. Consequently, the initial response to the Mau-Mau uprising was not coordinated. Laws proscribing the movement and forbidding people to take the Mau-Mau oath were promulgated, even making membership of the secret group a capital offence. To further address the effect of oath-taking, the government embarked on screening processes, during which a loyalty certificate was issued to those who had not taken an oath of allegiance to the Mau-Mau. This certificate would allow the recipient to work outside the local area; in contrast, those who had taken the oath would be denied the certificate and fined up to 100

LEFT **A mock attack enacted by the white settlers, with bamboo sticks used to guard farmhouses and farm labourers. (Courtesy of the Nicholas Wood Collection)**

shillings, with an additional penalty of around 20 shillings during the state of emergency. For many landless people, these were substantial amounts of money.

When these measures failed to stop the activities of the Mau-Mau, the colonial government reinforced the military effort to bring down the rebellion. The colonial security force can be divided into four parts, namely: the Kenyan Regiment, the King's African Rifles, the home guard and the Kenyan Police. The Kenyan Regiment was resident in the country as a paramilitary officer training battalion; the King's African Rifles was manned by Africans, and consisted of British and African non-commissioned officers, although the supervision was by Africans. The African troops were recruited from throughout the continent, including other parts of the British colonies. Indeed, the former Ugandan dictator, Idi Amin, was a member of the King's African Rifles who fought against the Mau-Mau in Kenya. The key battalions of the King's African Rifles that took part in the war were the 4th KAR from Uganda and the 6th KAR from Tanganyika. The home guard was comprised mainly of Africans who had converted to Christianity, and it became part of the security forces in May 1953. The Kenyan Police, for its part, was, like the King's African Rifles, composed mainly of Africans, with British police officers occupying key billets. The police played a key role in the colonial response to the insurgence. At the beginning of the revolt, the police had the following departments: Criminal Investigation Department, Inspection Department, Training Department, Department of Supply Services, Signals Branch and Special Branch. Until 1945, the Special Branch was part of the Criminal Investigation Department. It was the intelligence gathering section of the police and was charged with considerable responsibilities during the Mau-Mau revolt.

The first military operation was Operation *Jock Scott*, which was launched almost immediately after the emergency was declared in October 1952. The operation had the sole mission of arresting key members of the Mau-Mau, thereby curtailing the activities of the movement. The Lancashire Fusiliers were flown from the Suez Canal Zone to Nairobi, and they spent their first day parading the streets of

RIGHT **Kikuyu *askaris* disguised as farm labourers checking identification papers. It was a standard practice to perform random checking of identification papers, and black Kenyans had to have valid papers to enable free movement and obtain employment. (Courtesy of the Nicholas Wood Collection)**

Nairobi in a psychological exercise to encourage the whites and intimidate the Mau-Mau. Not much success, however, attended Operation *Jock Scott*. Mau-Mau oath-taking continued, and even increased. Indeed the government's main supporters – white settlers and African loyalists – were the chief critics of the operation.

A second military operation, *Anvil*, was launched between 24 April and 9 May 1954. This was a cordon and search operation of Nairobi involving four battalions of troops, and it was under the command of General Sir George Erskine, who had considerable experience in counter-insurgencies and was given full operations control of all colonial, auxiliary, police and security forces at the end of May 1953. This operation was more successful, especially in cutting off support for the Mau-Mau from the city. The attendant result was that the guerrillas were isolated in the forest for some time before they were able to organize other lines of support. The operation began at about 3am, with security agents surrounding key Kikuyu locations like Bahati, Makongeni, Ziwani, Kariokor and Pumwani. With exits blocked, those inside had no chance of escaping. However, from the accounts of former Mau-Mau guerrillas, information about the impending operation had been obtained through Mau-Mau agents working as part of the government security services. Consequently, many key Mau-Mau members had escaped from the areas, and those caught were mainly passive members of the movement or completely innocent people. Another operation, *Harmer*, was launched in January 1955. This lasted for three weeks, with over a division of infantry thrown into the Aberdare forest to flush out the Mau-Mau insurgents. Despite the massive nature of the operation, the government recorded only 161 dead, captured or surrendered.

ABOVE **Delaware Avenue, a prominent street in Nairobi during the Mau-Mau uprising. Every effort was made to ensure that areas like this were not penetrated by the Mau-Mau warriors. (Courtesy of the Nicholas Wood Collection)**

OPPOSITE **Bodies of killed Mau-Mau warriors being inspected by a member of the home guard. The open display of bodies of killed Mau-Mau soldiers was a psychological way of preventing people from joining the group. (Courtesy of the Nicholas Wood Collection)**

By this time, the government seemed to have come to the conclusion that the sheer weight and density of the government forces involved would not defeat the Mau-Mau, and that an unorthodox military tactic was required. Consequently, a number of guerrillas who had surrendered were converted and sent back into the forests to persuade their compatriots to surrender. This strategy of employing pseudo-gangs worked, and from this moment battle tides began to move against the Mau-Mau insurgents. This was not helped by the battle fatigue and internal division that were growing among the guerrillas. Shortly after employing this strategy, key members of the Mau-Mau were arrested, including General China. The arrest of General China was a turning point. After his arrest, he remained resolute, such that his interrogator noted that 'He was a complete fanatic [who] has no fear of execution. He is completely self exposing and cannot be convinced that Mau-Mau is doomed ... At the time of his interrogation, his sole wish was to expound his political testament and then walk to the gallows without trial.' After some time, though, he did a major U-turn and became a stalwart champion of the government's call on the Mau-Mau to surrender. In exchange for his life, he decided to negotiate the surrender of the more than 5,000 guerrillas under his command. Although this failed at the last minute, information already received from him about the inner workings of the Mau-Mau was of tremendous assistance to the security forces.

The colonial government also used psychological intimidation to bring down the rebellion. Those detained were given brutal punishment and some were, in fact, beaten to death by the home guards. This attracted global concern in March 1959, when 11 detainees at the Hola detention camp died. Although it was initially reported that they died from contaminated water, autopsies later showed that they had been beaten to death. The event led to protests in England and the institution of a commission of inquiry. In another exercise of psychological intimidation, a mobile gallows was transported around the country, dispensing justice to Mau-Mau suspects, while the government also employed the practice of displaying the bodies of slain guerrilla fighters to villagers as a warning, especially when they were 'generals' or senior members of the movement. For example, after General Kirita ole Kisio of Narok Masai and General Bata Batu of Mount Kenya Hika Hika Battalion were killed, their bodies were publicly displayed. Draconian laws were also introduced to forestall people from taking active parts in the Mau-Mau rebellion. The death penalty was imposed for possession of guns and ammunition, and for administering oaths. The government also introduced communal punishments whereby, in cases of serious Mau-Mau incidents, whole communities of Africans were evicted. For example, after the killing of a European in Leshau, 4,324 Kikuyus were expelled. In addition, 300 Kikuyus were evicted in Ndosura village after another incident, and a case of arson in Solai saw 80 people banished to the Reserve.

There were other cases of brutality in the Mau-Mau detention camps. Accounts by Kenyan and European authors have confirmed that many Mau-Mau detainees suffered considerably in the hands of home guards and British troops. This brutality also extended to women and children. There were cases of children left alone in a detention camp while their mothers were working. What, however, ignited opposition in the eyes of the British public were statements that children as young as 11 were sentenced to solitary confinement for singing Mau-Mau songs. This allegation of child abuse was taken up by Labour MPs in the House of Commons, and the Colonial Secretary was forced to admit that an 'error' had been made in sentencing children under the legal age of 14.

This brutality was inflicted on arrested Mau-Mau suspects in order to force them to admit that they had taken the oath and to supply information about the inner workings of the movement. While some cooperated, others remained defiant, and many others gave completely wrong information, embellishing their stories in ways that they knew would convince their captors that they were giving an accurate account. But by the time the number of arrests increased, it was

ABOVE **Nairobi streets in 1953–54. The desire to take control of government in the city was a major cause of the Mau-Mau rebellion. (Courtesy of the Nicholas Wood Collection)**

clear that the days of the Mau-Mau rebellion were numbered, and that the membership was dwindling.

THE END OF THE MAU-MAU REVOLT

By mid-1956, the number of Mau-Mau arrests had begun to increase. Dedan Kimathi himself was arrested on 21 October 1956. The arrest of Dedan Kimathi can be taken to mark the end of the operational phase of the Mau-Mau. Why the rebellion failed has been the subject of discussion in several quarters. But an attendant question is whether the revolt did actually fail. If the intention was to force the Europeans out of Kenya and obtain independence for the country exclusively through this process, then the Mau-Mau may be considered to have fallen short. However, if the goal was to force the colonial power to appreciate the futility of continued colonial control of the country and to caution the settlers against contemplating unilateral independence like the one then being rumoured to be in the offing, then the entire insurgent operation was a success. Considering it exclusively as a military machine, the Mau-Mau collapsed as a result of several factors, including the extent of the force that the colonial power brought to bear on the rebellion, the series of internal fights that broke out among the key members of the movement, battle weariness that was beginning to affect many members of the guerrilla force, strategic lack of foresight and proper education.

The extent of the military firepower that was brought to bear on the Mau-Mau was such that the guerrillas had no chance of securing military victory. The troops sent in to fight the Mau-Mau were of such sophistication that an irregular force could never succeed. But without doubt the main reason for the collapse of the Mau-Mau war machine

RIGHT **The Langata camp. One of the detention camps built for suspected Mau-Mau insurgents. A policeman stands by, overlooking suspected rebels.** (Courtesy of topfoto.co.uk)

56

was the differences among key members of the force. First, disagreements soon began to emerge between those who were educated and the illiterates, with the latter accusing Dedan Kimathi and other educated leaders of using the advantage of their literacy to browbeat them into conformity. At the centre of this opposition was Mathenge, whom many of the illiterate members of the Mau-Mau considered as their leader. It is noteworthy that Mathenge was the only Mau-Mau commander who refused to take any 'commissioned' rank, a decision that won him affection and loyalty from many of the uneducated segments of the organization, who saw the luxuriant ranks of the other commanders as symbols of the feudal tendencies they were fighting in the British colonial rule. The anti-education group later formed the *Riigi*. At a later stage in the struggle, the *Riigi* were to enter into some surrendering arrangements with the government.

Over time, too, differences began to emerge over targets of attack. For example, around August 1953, Kimathi had suggested that more raids should be made into the Rift Valley, where there were considerable white farmlands. Many of the generals, however, lacked enthusiasm, as the area was particularly unfamiliar and there was the risk of starvation there. But it has also been suggested that there were more personal reasons for the refusal to support Kimathi's position, as many of the leaders preferred to remain in the Central province, which was closer to their homes and also offered them opportunity for access to women and other pleasures in life. Kimathi also had fundamental disagreements with General China. Internal squabbles continued among the guerrillas. The lowest point was reached when Kimathi ordered the arrest of Kenya *Riigi* leaders. Although they were caught and arrested, they eventually escaped.

The arrest of General China by the security agencies brought its own attendant problems for the Mau-Mau. Kimathi totally opposed General China's surrender call. He was more in favour of peace talks than surrender talk. After General China's change in position, the Mau-Mau

LEFT **A mock attack to prepare the government security agents for Mau-Mau activities. This operation is being undertaken jointly by the white officers and black members of the home guard. (Courtesy of the Nicholas Wood Collection)**

had to consider a total overhaul in strategy, as they thought that China would have revealed all the movement's strategies to the government. There were grounds for this belief, as the government was able to destroy most of the Mau-Mau communications and supplies and arrest many of the passive wing of the Mau-Mau.

But some of the reasons for the failure also lay within the Mau-Mau strategy. First, the idea of oath was largely Kikuyu, and it was not popular with other ethnic groups. Many thought that a more flexible oath, adapted to suit all Kenya Africans, would have been more appropriate. Another reason for isolation was the view held by many members that it was a Kikuyu struggle, and that the reward of victory, including high positions in future government, would be monopolized. Even in cases where members of other ethnic groups volunteered to join the Mau-Mau, after they had benefited from the activities of the movement, as in the case of some of the prisoners released after the prison raid, they were still refused membership on the grounds that they were not Kikuyus. Memoirs written by ex-Mau-Mau soldiers noted that the strategy of exclusion which the Mau-Mau preached was, with the advantage of hindsight, a major mistake. Mohamed Mathu explains further:

One of the Prisoners [we had recently released] asked if he might join the group. A few of us thought it was all right, but Kariuku rejected the idea because the man was a Luo. 'This is a Kikuyu struggle,' he said, as most of the others nodded their heads in approval, 'and we don't want any Luo to have claims on us after the victory is won.' I felt this was a very narrow view. It was an 'African' as well as 'Kikuyu' struggle we were engaged in; why weaken ourselves by rejecting the help of other tribes? Looking back, I think this type of thing did much to destroy our chances of success.

Nature was also believed to have played its part in the Mau-Mau surrender. The crop harvest around the time combined with the hardship of the communal labour schemes to create a starvation that cautioned against continued fighting against the superior firepower of the British government.

Without deriding the leadership of the Mau-Mau, there is also no doubt that lack of education was a crucial factor in the defeat of the movement. With the arrest and detention of many educated members immediately after the declaration of the state of emergency, the management of the group fell into the hands of people who lacked political experience, education and the knowledge of warfare necessary for the success of a popular revolution. Although strong and resolute in their determination, there was a limit to what they could achieve without proper educational backing to supply a more meaningful framework for their rebellion. As time went on, the struggle needed more strength to propel it beyond bold determination, and in this case the Mau-Mau warriors could not provide it, especially as the bulk of the leadership that could furnish it with intellectual backing had been arrested and imprisoned. By the time it ended, the cost of the entire rebellion was: Mau-Mau: 11,503 killed, 2,585 captured; government forces: 63 Europeans, 3 Asians, 101 Africans killed and 101 Europeans, 12 Asians, 1,469 African wounded; civilians: 1,819 Africans, 32 Europeans, 26 Asians killed, and 916 Africans, 26 Europeans, 36 Asians wounded. Financially, the cost of the emergency was £55,585,424.

CONCLUSION

No other struggle against colonial rule in Africa has attracted such controversy and interest as the Mau-Mau revolt in Kenya. Apart from being the first organized African military activity to aspire to political independence, it also had the unique distinction of being the only anti-

LEFT **Residence of a white family, with a special wire fence to protect the bedroom from night-time attacks; the Mau-Mau insurgents often attacked at night. (Courtesy of the Nicholas Wood Collection)**

colonial struggle that was undertaken without any recourse to external assistance. Indeed, subsequent independence struggles in Namibia, Angola, Mozambique, Rhodesia and South Africa sought and obtained inspiration from the determination of the bunch of irregular soldiers that took on the might of the British imperial force. What exactly the Mau-Mau was would remain a matter of opinion. While some continue to see the group as a bunch of rascals that killed and maimed innocent people, others, especially Kenyans, see the whole rebellion as a revolutionary expression of a national sentiment, whose unorthodox methods misled the colonial government at the time, and are still misleading some of its recent theorists.

Militarily, the Mau-Mau warriors were, of course, no match for the British forces. Apart from sophisticated arms, the latter also had the numerical advantage and could use other means to intimidate the population into submission. But the Mau-Mau warriors believed that with a just cause and a sacred struggle they could attract international attention to their cause, even if they sometimes did so in negative ways. Consequently, they fought the colonial government with all the strength at their disposal. Much has been said about the advantage the Mau-Mau possessed because of the knowledge of their environment. While this cannot be doubted, it should also be noted that life in the bush was often tough, and thus required determination and conviction. The fact that many survived was due to their remarkable courage and resourcefulness. Even one of their worst enemies, Ian Henderson, the police officer who was at the forefront of most of the police operations against the Mau-Mau, commended their 'bush-craft' as being of superlative standards, when he confirmed that they were able to run in the forest 'at staggering speed'.

Although the Mau-Mau revolt failed in its basic objective of expelling the British, one success of the entire enterprise was that it set the path for a meaningful decolonization dialogue for Kenya. Indeed, before the revolt, there were rumours that some of the white settlers in Kenya were

RIGHT **Mau-Mau warriors, including children, emerging from the forest after the independence of Kenya in 1963. Some Mau-Mau fighters remained loyal to their oath that they would come out of the forest only after the country gained its independence.** (Courtesy of topfoto.co.uk)

contemplating unilateral independence, something similar to what was later undertaken by Ian Smith in Rhodesia. It was even said that some of them had contacted South African Premier Malan for assistance towards unilateral independence. With the Mau-Mau revolt, it became clear that continued colonial occupation of Kenya would be an expensive enterprise. Consequently, the path to independence of the East African nation began.

While the Mau-Mau rebellion could be said to have ended with the arrest of Dedan Kimathi and the surrender of the bulk of Mau-Mau insurgents in the Mount Kenya and Aberdare forests, there still remained a hard core of Mau-Mau fighters who remained loyal to their oath not to return from the forest until the day Kenya was free from colonial control. On Kenya's Independence Day, these people came out of the forests and entered the independence parade arena to the warm admiration and respect of their countrymen. Although they were battered and bruised, they still remained erect and unbeaten. To date, Mau-Mau legacies still remain a key issue in Kenya. While the generation of those who fought in the war is dwindling fast, the few still alive remember their years in the forest with nostalgic pathos, arguing, as one would expect, that they gave their best amidst overwhelming odds.

GLOSSARY

askari:	Swahili word for security guard
Batuni:	first of the oaths taken by the Mau-Mau fighters
bhangi:	a local drug often taken by Mau-Mau warriors
gatheci:	literally 'a sharp instrument'. However, during the Mau-Mau war, the word was used to describe the African home guards, because they were initially armed with spears
Gikuyu na Mumbi:	the mythical father of the Kikuyu ethnic group and his wife, Mumbi
gitete:	a small gourd
gutahiko:	de-oathing process organized by the government for those who had taken the Mau-Mau oath
kiama:	council of elders
Kirinyaga:	Kikuyu term for Mount Kenya
Komerara:	a term used for criminals hiding from the law. During the Mau-Mau war, it was used for those who joined the struggle as an escape opportunity from the law. Such people were often in the forest to steal from the peasants' farms. They were considered to be unhelpful to the long-term Mau-Mau cause
Kuri hono-i ndirara	literally meaning 'It is cold, where shall I sleep?' This was a forest signal to camp guards indicating that one was not an enemy
Mei Mathathi army:	Mount Kenya guerrillas, under the leadership of General China. 'Mei'

	means Meru, Embu and Ikamba, the three groups that made up the majority of Mount Kenya fighters
miraa:	drugs taken by the Mau-Mau guerrillas
Muiguithania:	the Unifier
Muingi:	name for the Mau-Mau Movement
muma:	oath
Muma wa Ngero:	Oath of Violence
Muma wa Uiguano:	Oath of Unity
mundu muga wa ita:	medicine man who made battle predictions for the Mau-Mau
mzungu:	white man
Ngai:	Kikuyu name for God
ngworu:	stomach contents of a goat employed in purification ceremonies
nja ya ita:	war council
nyapara:	foreman or farm overseer
Nyomu Nditu:	literally 'the heavy forest'. It was a forest term used to describe the Mau-Mau
panga:	a long, curved knife sharpened on one side; introduced by the Europeans
settlers:	originally a term used for white foreigners, it was later applied to all the enemies of the Mau-Mau, including Asians and Africans
tie-tie:	word of derision for Africans who always tried to look and behave like Europeans, especially by putting on ties and dressing like them
Uhuru:	Swahili word for Swahili
Uiguano:	unity

BIBLIOGRAPHY

Barnett, Donald L. and Njama, Karari, *Mau-Mau from Within: Autobiography and Analysis of Kenya's Peasant Revolt*, Macgibbon and Kee Ltd, London (1966)

Buijtenhuijs, Rob, *Essay on Mau-Mau: Contribution to Mau-Mau Historiography*, African Studies Centre: Research Report No. 17/1982

Furedi, Frank, *Mau-Mau War in Perspective,* James Currey, London (1989)

Kabiro, Ngugi, *Man in the Middle*, LSM Information Centre, Richmond, Canada (1973)

Kanogo, Tabitha, *Squatters and the Roots of Mau-Mau, 1905–1963,* James Currey, London (1987)

Kenyatta, Jomo, *Facing Mount Kenya: The Tribal Life of the Kikuyu*, Mecurity Books, London (1965)

Leakey, L.S.B., *Mau-Mau and the Kikuyu*, Methuen & Co, London (1952)

Maloba, Wunyabari, *Mau-Mau and Kenya*, James Currey, Oxford (1998)

Marshall, Macphee, *Kenya*, Ernest Benn Limited, London (1967)

Mathu, Mohammed, *The Urban Guerrilla*, LSM Information Centre, Richmond, Canada (1974)

Wa Wanjou, Gakaara, *Mau-Mau Author in Detention,* Heinemann, Nairobi (1988)

Wunyabati, Maloba, *Mau Mau and Kenya: Analyses of a Peasant Revolt*, Kenya, East African Educational Publisher (1994)

COLOUR PLATE COMMENTARY

A: MAU-MAU WARRIOR

A typical Mau-Mau warrior often had a mixture of traditional and western weapons. This peculiar pattern of armament was determined by the nature of the war. The basic weapons available to most Mau-Mau warriors were shield **(1)**, long spear **(2)**, sword, *simi* **(3)** or long-sword and, notoriously, the *panga* **(4)**. These could be procured locally, and indeed many Kikuyu males owned them, as they had used them in inter-group conflicts even before the arrival of colonial rule. The shield was often made of animal skins. Most of the time the Mau-Mau warriors also had a small knife close to their chests. This was to assist in close-range fighting with members of the security forces. Increasingly, however, the Mau-Mau fighters had access to guns, and this enhanced their operations. The guns and ammunition came from a variety of sources, including thefts, captures and purchases from Asians and even European businessmen. There were also locally made guns **(5)**, but these were known to have disappointed at crucial times.

B: INITIATION OATH

The initiation oath was undoubtedly one of the most crucial aspects of the Mau-Mau movement. This marked the formal entrance into the fold. The initiation ceremony often took place at night inside a room or deep in the forest. The new member would be asked to remove his shoes and all metal coins in his pockets. The process of initiation included the slaughtering of a goat, whose meat would be roasted and later used as part of the initiation materials. The new convert was then made to kneel down, holding a piece of meat on one hand, with the other hand holding a liquid concoction. He took the meat, and drank the liquid content in the bowl as he recited the oathing declarations in the hearing of the initiator and other people present.

BELOW **Black Kenyans queuing to be photographed before being issued with passes. Stringent questioning often preceded the issue of these passes. (Courtesy of the Nicholas Wood Collection)**

C: TRAINING SESSION

The training of Mau-Mau warriors was undertaken by Mau-Mau leaders, some of whom had experience fighting alongside British troops in Burma during World War II. The main training camps were in the Aberdare and Mount Kenya forests, and gave instruction in the use of guns, laying ambushes and hit-and-run operations. They also provided an opportunity to teach the members other civic duties they should hold for the Kikuyu cause. There was minimal training in the use of spears and other traditional weapons, as these were weapons with which the insurgents were very familiar. Over time, the training session came to include marching, parades, inspection of the guard of honour and other elements expected of a conventional military force. Rank allocations were also made along the lines of conventional military structure, with the supreme rank of Field Marshal reserved for very senior commanders.

D: PRISON RAID

Attacks on secluded government installations such as this prison were a major element in Mau-Mau strategy, and raids on prisons played a key part in acquiring weapons and freeing prisoners who, depending on whether or not they were members of the Kikuyu ethnic group, might be allowed to join the Mau-Mau. These raids involved a sudden attack on the security guards. The numbers of guerrilla insurgents making such attacks were often high enough to overpower the guards. After such raids, Mau-Mau guerrillas often escaped with weapons and ammunition recovered from the security guards stationed at the prison yards.

E: CLASH WITH AUTHORITIES

Mau-Mau direct attacks on government security forces involved the guerrillas laying ambushes for the security forces. The guerrillas were often armed with spears and machetes, with some of them holding guns, while the government security forces frequently had guns. Although the superior weapons of the security forces often placed them at an advantage, with Mau-Maus suffering enormous losses, sometimes the insurgents were nevertheless able to inflict considerable casualties.

F: MAU-MAU TRIAL

After the government proscribed Mau-Mau, membership of the organization and taking part in oathing ceremonies became offences punishable by death. Once arrested, the accused person was tried in a court, from where, after conviction, he would be taken to the gallows to be hanged. Courtrooms were sometimes arranged in such a way that the gallows would be visible to the accused person in the dock. An African security force would often guard the accused person throughout the trial.

BELOW **Mau-Mau suspects behind barbed wire, with armed security guards patrolling to ensure compliance with instructions. (Courtesy of topfoto.co.uk)**

INDEX

References to illustrations are shown in **bold**. Plates are shown with page and caption locators in brackets.